Battered Women as Survivors

Battered Women as Survivors

An Alternative to Treating
Learned Helplessness

Edward W. Gondolf
Western Psychiatric Institute and Clinic
University of Pittsburgh

with
Ellen R. Fisher
Austin Center for Battered Women

Lexington Books
D.C. Heath and Company/Lexington, Massachusetts/Toronto

Library of Congress Cataloging-in-Publication Data

Gondolf, Edward W., 1948-
    Battered women as survivors : an alternative to treating learned helplessness / Edward
W. Gondolf with Ellen R. Fisher.
          p.   cm.
    Includes index.
    ISBN 0-669-18166-8 (alk. paper)
    1. Abused women—Services for—Texas—Case studies. 2. Women's shelters—Texas—Case
studies. 3. Abused wives—Texas—Psychology—Case studies. 4. Social work with women—
Texas—Case studies.
I. Fisher, Ellen R. II. Title.
HV1446.T4G65   1988   362.8'3—dc 19   88-8085

Published simultaneously in Canada
Printed in the United States of America
International Standard Book Number: 0-669-18166-8
Library of Congress Catalog Card Number: 88-8085

The paper used in this publication meets the minimum requirements of American National
Standard for Information Sciences—Permanence of Paper for Printed Library Materials,
ANSI Z39.48-1984. ∞™

89 90 91 92 8 7 6 5 4 3 2

Contents

List of Tables and Figures

Tables

Figures

Acknowledgments

T his book had rather serendipitous beginnings. I happened to meet Ellen Fisher and Debbie Tucker of the Texas Council on Family Violence at the Third International Institute on Victimology. During the week of presentations, we found ourselves discussing what we felt were shortcomings of the research in the field. Little of the research seemed to address specifically the program and intervention issues facing practitioners in the field.

Ellen Fisher and I, with Debbie Tucker's support, vowed then to pool our resources and skills to conduct some research of our own. We planned to analyze the shelter data that the Texas Council on Family Violence had been collecting. Ellen brought valuable experience working in state-level administration and as director of one of the leading shelters in Texas. She assisted with the initial conception of the research, proper release of the data, and consultation throughout the analysis. I was able to contribute research skills as a sociologist and my knowledge of men who batter as a counselor in a program for batterers. I then analyzed the data and wrote the research report. The partnership has made for what we consider to be an ideal model of collaboration between practitioner and researcher, and between women's shelter and men's program workers.

I owe a great deal of thanks to the many other individuals who contributed to the development of this project. Lee Bowker, the former dean of the Indiana University of Pennsylvania (IUP) Graduate School, provided encouragement and resources for the initial phases of the research. It was, in fact, his noted study, *Beating Wife Beating* (1983), that stirred my initial interest in researching the helpseeking topic. A faculty research grant under the subsequent dean, David Lynch, helped to continue the project. Rick McFerron, director of Academic Computing Services at IUP, assisted with data management and computation.

A number of people at the University of Pittsburgh, where I am currently a research fellow, also deserve my appreciation. My colleagues Ed Mulvey, Chuck Lidz, and Kathy Woodard provided much advice on the analysis and a supportive setting in which to accomplish it. I thank too the director of Clinical Services Research, Herbert Schulberg, for his endorsement and support of the project. Much of the analysis and reporting was completed under an NIMH research fellowship (NIMH T32 MH17184) at the Western Psychiatric Institute and Clinic of the University of Pittsburgh.

Most important, there are the many people of Texas who made this book possible. I thank Debbie Tucker and Melissa Eddy, of the Texas Council on Family Violence, and Kate Refern, of the Texas Department of Human Services, for their valuable assistance. And we all extend appreciation to the many Texas shelter staff and battered women who generously completed the questionnaires during a time of crisis. We take great courage from their efforts to end the violence against women, and hope that in some small way this book adds to their momentum.

1
Introduction

The Psychologizing of Wife Abuse

Shifts in the Shelter Movement

The battered-women shelter movement is one of our modern miracles. In fifteen years' time, a thousand shelters and major legislation have replaced the virtual ignorance of wife abuse (Schechter 1982). This is an accomplishment matched only by the settlement house movement at the turn of the century.

With little or no government support, and oftentimes with intense citizen and professional opposition, grass-roots women's groups gave birth to shelters. Women of many backgrounds and orientations were united in a way that eventually brought shelters legitimacy and respect from the community at large. But like many similar movements, the initial activism has gradually given way to a more professional posture—and with it has come a different conception of battered women.[1]

Wife abuse was introduced as a feminist issue—that is, an issue that demonstrated the secondary status of women in American society.[2] Wife abuse, in the feminist view, was the result of the patriarchy and sexist attitudes that degraded and oppressed women. It was a deeply embedded social problem that had to be redressed with social change—change that brought greater equality and status to women in general. Battered women, therefore, needed not only care and emotional support but also to be made aware of the social circumstances of their abuse. They needed ultimately to be "empowered"— that is, mobilized to challenge their subjection and take charge of their lives (Penz 1981).

From these feminist and activist beginnings, wife abuse increasingly became a humanist issue. Family service and mental health professionals gradually brought their clinical expertise to bear on wife abuse, but not without depoliticizing it and psychologizing abuse in the process (Pleck 1987; Tierney 1982). The abuse "victim" has consequently become a new population to "treat," rather than advocate for or empower. Therapists and counselors look more for psychological deficiencies and ailments in the victim to redress and make better (Dobash and Dobash 1981).

Factors within the shelter movement have also contributed to this shift in emphasis. The shelter movement was essentially founded on the notion that building an "alternate community" for isolated battered women was a "treatment" in itself. Some battered women, however, appeared to resist this feminist approach, and nearly half of the women in shelters returned to their batterers (Ferraro 1982). Many shelters consequently attempted to accommodate the women as "clients" by developing more clinical services. Also, increased pressure for funds and accountability forced many shelters to adopt a more conventional agency structure. Many of these shelters have evolved into multiservice centers with professional staff assuming leadership in place of grass-roots volunteers and activists (Pleck 1987).

There have, of course, been some gains in the process as well as some losses. The most obvious gain is the expansion of assistance offered to a large number and diversity of women. The main loss is that a severe social and political problem has been transformed into a psychological one. Practitioners are increasingly identifying the problem of wife abuse as "in" the victim and treating it with psychotherapies. As a recent study in *Social Work* documents (Davis 1987), the discussion of the clinical diagnosis and psychological treatment of battered women had dramatically increased over the last five years, and the characterization of battered women has accordingly changed.

Shortcomings in Community Services

This book presents research that empirically counters much of the existing trend and substantiates the initial social analysis of battered women. It examines in particular the helpseeking behavior of shelter women in Texas. That is, it considers battered women's efforts to contact various help sources in response to their abuse. Over six thousand intake and exit interviews of women in all fifty Texas shelters (during an eighteen-month period) were analyzed to derive our findings. (See appendix for more on the methodology.)

In our research, shelter women do not appear to display the "victim" characteristics commonly ascribed to those who are battered. They appear instead as "survivors," acting assertively and logically in response to the abuse. They contact a variety of "help sources," from friends and relatives to social services and the police, but with little result. The deficiencies seem, therefore, to be in the helping sources to which the women appeal and confide.

This study consequently turns out to be more about "us," the helpers, service providers, and policymakers, rather than about "them," the so-called victims of domestic violence. An examination of the shelter women's helpseeking behavior inevitably exposes the "helpgiving" behavior, particularly of our "community services" designed to aid battered women—shelters, social services, and police.

The study in fact adds to the merging direction of recent research that is beginning to investigate what's wrong with the interventions, rather than with the battered woman. It is only recently that studies, such as Lee Bowker's (1983) *Beating Wife Beating*, have begun to seriously examine our intervention programs and policies. Some critics have suggested that our inattentiveness in this regard may be a reflection of the same sexism that delayed the "discovery" of the abuse problem.

Most of the research of the past has been preoccupied with the incidence, nature, and causes of abuse. The repeated question "Why do battered women return to their batterers?" has been answered largely with studies of the woman's dependencies on the man. Deficiencies in the women are exposed in the process and treatment recommended for them.

The real questions, however, may lie with our interventions and services. How do they allow for such severe abuse to continue? Should safety be a fundamental right in our society sustained and maintained by public services? Extreme security measures are imposed in airports to curtail terrorist attack or bombing. Government officials vow to apprehend and prosecute terrorists. Yet the response to epidemic terror in the home is minimal. Practitioners lament that there is not much more they can do because of the "learned helplessness" in the victim (Walker 1979).

Besides raising questions about the shortcomings in our social services, our study addresses the prevailing notion of "learned helplessness" in battered women. Learned helplessness suggests that battered women are basically passive and submissive in response to abuse. It is a notion, however, that appears to be rooted in assumptions and observations rather than hard fact. The theoretical presentation for our study offers a kind of "sociology of knowledge" by discussing how the notion of learned helplessness was established and posing an alternative conception to take its place.

Our study also leads to some fundamental queries about human nature that go beyond the status of battered women. What is it about women in general that enables them to survive amidst such adversity? Are there innate capabilities and resiliencies that we have failed to adequately acknowledge and explore? We suggest that battered women demonstrate tremendous resiliency, persistence, and strength which press for a less pathological orientation to "victims." As the title suggests, we believe their experience points to an alternate characterization—one that considers battered women fundamentally as "survivors."

Format of the Book

Overview

The remainder of this introductory chapter outlines the methodology of our study and describes our sample of Texas shelter women. It notes, in particular, that battered women have suffered from the severest kinds of abuse and from poverty and limited mobility as well. Chapter 2 elaborates our "survivor hypothesis" and specifically contrasts it with the learned helplessness theory that has dominated the conceptions of and response to battered women. Chapter 3 summarizes the women's helpseeking behavior prior to coming to the shelter and presents an empirical model to illustrate our survivor hypothesis.

In chapter 4, we attempt to apply our survivor hypothesis to different kinds of battered women. We discuss in particular the role that race and shelter status have in differentiating battered women. Our data suggest that the level of helpseeking remains relatively constant among racial groups, and that an emerging category of nonresident shelter women have sought less help but have more resources and less severe abuse.

Chapter 5 turns to the source of the problem—the men who batter—and in the process exposes some of the shortcomings in our interventions with wife abuse. The data analysis presented here suggests that there are different types of batterers. Two types that stand out are the sociopathic and antisocial batterers who have been violent outside the home, been previously arrested, and severely abuse drugs and alcohol. The women appear to respond to these batterers with more helpseeking, as our hypothesis suggests. In this chapter we also report on the police action used to intervene in the men's battering. The police appear, according to our study, to be reacting more to the antisocial behavior of the men than to the severity of wife abuse.

Chapter 6 considers the role of shelters in furthering the helpseeking process. It begins with a summary of the shelter services women obtain as shelter residents and the shelter services they expect to continue after leaving the shelter. The impact of shelter service is considered next. The analysis affirms that an increase in resources that afford greater independence do in fact contribute to a woman's leaving the batterer. One cautionary sidelight: The batterer's being in counseling is one of the strongest predictors of a woman's returning to the batterer.

Lastly, we offer a summary and conclusion in chapter 7. This chapter restates the findings that describe and explain the helpseeking behavior of the shelter women, and then discusses the implications of these findings for shelters, community services, and social policy. In essence, an integrated system of community interventions is needed to assure a decisive interruption of the violence and sufficient resources to enable the battered women to live independently from the batterer. This chapter also outlines means to address the principal barrier to achieving this ideal, namely, the learned helplessness within our community services.

Our Use of Statistics

This book attempts to bridge the technical world of researchers and the practical orientation of practitioners. In the process, it admittedly poses some shortcomings to both audiences, as well as some contributions. Much of the methodological discussion has been relegated to notes appearing at the end of each chapter or to the appendix.

The contents of the book remain somewhat technical, nevertheless. We believe it is necessary at this point within the field to offer further empirical study of the fundamental assumptions about battered women. Therefore, we include in each chapter an overview of the existing empirical research on the topic at hand, a brief description of the method of analysis, a summary of the findings, and finally a discussion of the implications of that particular analysis. Those less interested in the technical details of the research may want to focus on chapters 2 and 7 and perhaps review the concluding section of each chapter.

The field has in fact relied extensively on clinical observations, qualitative interview studies, and polemical essays in shaping its concepts and interventions. While this basis provides a vivid portrayal of the nature of abuse and confronts us with the harsh reality of real people, it overlooks the scope and differentiation of abuse and women's response to it. The more qualitative approach thus allows undocumented or untested generalizations to develop.

The empirical basis of this book serves, therefore, several important purposes for the practitioner. One, it offers a context by which to weigh and sort one's individual hunches and observations. This is particularly useful given the emotionally charged and crisis-oriented settings in which most practitioners find themselves.

Two, the empirical base of statistics enables us to develop generalizations about a category of individuals. These generalizations are vital to formulating meaningful policy and effective programs that, by their very nature, must address large groups of people. Three, many of the statistics presented here are an attempt to move beyond descriptive bivariate analysis to a more explanatory multivariate analysis that suggests "why" as well as "what" is going on. In the process, patterns and associations are discovered that are not readily apparent in everyday observations.

In sum, we endeavor in the writing that follows to establish some much needed hard evidence, but also to bring it down off the shelf, so to speak, and into the hands of practitioners who most need it. We hope in the process to enliven the debate about how to characterize and assist battered women, and thus help redirect a field drifting from its roots.

Sample Description

While statistical descriptions in themselves often blunt the experience and tragedy of wife abuse, they may at times also serve as a harsh reminder of its extent and severity. The statistics from our sample of more than six thousand women do in fact act in this way. They portray a group of women severely, extensively, and cruelly assaulted that cannot be blandly relegated to another policy or treatment category. Moreover, it becomes evident that the Texas women also suffer from social burdens that compound their abuse and limit the possibility of their escaping it.

Abuse. The physical abuse inflicted on the Texas women appears to be more severe than for the other major samples of battered women: Bowker's (1983) study of "formerly battered" women, Pagelow's (1981) study of California shelter women, Stacey and Shupe's (1983) study of Dallas shelter women, and Walker's (1984) study of Rocky Mountain battered women (see table 1–1).[3] Forty-one percent of the Texas women had been abused with weapons or objects; 16 percent with a gun, and 17 percent with a knife. Additionally, two-thirds (67 percent) of the batterers had threatened to kill their victims. In the Stacey and Shupe (1983) sample of Dallas battered women discussed in *The*

Table 1–1
Abuse Experienced by Texas Sample

Physical Abuse	
Things thrown	46%
Held against will	69
Woman thrown around	83
Slapped	81
Pulled hair	61
Choked	57
Burned	9
Punched	75
Kicked	60
Weapon used	43
Verbal Abuse	
Personal insult	93
Threatened physical harm	77
Threatened sexual abuse	20
Threatened to use weapons	47
Threatened to kill	70
Threatened to harm child	42
Duration of Abuse	
First time	3
1 to 4 weeks	7
1 to 12 months	25
1 to 5 years	41
More than 5 years	24
Frequency of Abuse (During last 6 months)	
Only once	11
Once a month or less	24
2 to 3 a month	20
Once a week	12
2 to 6 a week	18
Daily	15

Family Secret, only 21 percent reported being abused with a weapon. Nearly three-quarters (72 percent) of our Texas sample were punched and over half (58 percent) kicked at some time. Other kinds of abuse were inflicted as well: sexual abuse (27 percent), pregnancy abuse (53 percent), and child abuse (56 percent). The wife abuse had been occurring for a year or more in 65 percent of the cases, in 24 percent of the cases for more than five years (74 percent and 26 percent respectively in the Stacey and Shupe sample).

The physical abuse caused head injuries for half (51 percent) of the Texas women and broken bones for 13 percent of the sample. Forty-two percent sought medical care for their injuries at some time during the relationship; 10 percent required hospitalization. Interestingly, more of our sample reported receiving bruises and cuts than the Stacey and Shupe sample, but fewer reported broken bones. An indicator of the psychological impact may be the portion of women who attempted suicide: this was 14 percent of our sample.

The abuse appears to come largely from generally violent or criminally prone batterers, as Walker (1983) and Stacey and Shupe (1983) have observed. Over one-third of the Texas batterers (37 percent) had abused people outside the home. In fact, 15 percent of the sample had been arrested for assault against nonfamily members. The overall arrest rate (56 percent) was, however, much less than the Walker sample (71 percent) and the Stacey and Shupe sample (81 percent). The majority of the Texas men (62 percent) reportedly had alcohol problems as well.

Background. Our sample also has a greater percentage of undereducated and underemployed women than the other studies of battered women (see table 1–2). This finding might reflect the disproportionate number of Texas shelter women from minority, lower working class, and larger sized families. For example, nearly half of the Texas women had only some high school education, as opposed to 39 percent of the Stacey and Shupe sample, 32 percent of the Pagelow sample, and 29 percent for the national average. The majority of the women's husbands (75 percent) made $15,000 or less a year, contrasting to 69 percent in the Stacey and Shupe sample and to a $15,000 average in the Walker sample and $23,000 average in the Bowker sample. Notably, 30 percent of the Texas batterers were currently unemployed. (Only 15 percent of the Stacey and Shupe sample and 14 percent of the Walker sample were unemployed.) Only 54 percent of the women were white, in contrast to 64 percent of the Stacey and Shupe sample, 80 percent of the Walker sample, and 78 percent of the Pagelow sample.

Reliability. The Texas shelter women do not, therefore, appear to be representative of all shelter women or of battered women in the state at large. They are, as mentioned, generally lower in income and more severely abused than other shelter and nonshelter samples of abused women. The Texas shelter

Table 1–2
Background of Texas Sample

Income (woman only)	
none	58%
$5,000 or less	20
$5,000–$10,000	12
10,001–$15,000	7
15,001–$20,000	4
Occupation (woman)	
Homemaker	55
Unskilled labor	15
Student	2
Clerical	9
Skilled labor	10
Manager/professional	6
Other	5
Education	
Less than 12 years	44
High school graduate/GED	37
Vocational training	4
College	15
Number of Children[a]	
None	11
One	27
Two	29
Three	20
Four	9
Five or more	5
Length of Relationship	
Less than one year	16
1 to 5 years	48
More than 5 years	36

[a]$\bar{x} = 2.0$

sample is also lower in socioeconomic status, higher in severity of abuse, and higher in helpseeking than a statewide survey derived from Texas driver's license holders ($N = 2000$ with a response rate of 60.5 percent) (Teske and Parker 1983).[4] (See appendix for discussion of yearly, regional, and urban–rural comparisons.)

These comparative samples may, however, be skewed in the other direction because of the selection process used to derive them. Many lower income women may have chosen not to participate in the other self-selection samples, or they may not have been aware of studies like Bowker's (1983, 1986) that recruited subjects largely through newspaper and magazine advertisements. Many of the lower income women, particularly the Hispanic women without citizenship, may not have had licenses. Therefore, they would have been omitted from the Texas driver's license sample. In fact, over half of our sample did not own a car.

We would expect, nevertheless, that the lower income status of our sample would work against the results we obtain rather than inflate them; previous helpseeking studies in the mental health field have in fact shown lower income and minority persons to be the least likely to seek formal help (chapter 4). The sample, in this light, offers an ideal "test case" for our helpseeking research.

The Texas shelter women do, moreover, represent an important starting point. The Texas sample represents a convincing proportion of battered women in the sheer numbers of the sample. It also represents the substantial numbers of battered women who have arrived "at our doorstep," so to speak. These are women who are looking for help and clearly need help. Their presence therefore begs our response. Just what form that response should take remains, as we suggest at the outset, somewhat unclear. But as the response to these battered women is improved, we can better serve other battered women, as well.

Notes

1. The shift described here does not mean to suggest that the feminist activism that initiated the shelter movement has been eliminated or suppressed. Feminism remains a vital, motivating force within the shelter movement. It is safe to say, however, that the radical voice of feminism is not as influential as it once was.

2. The term "wife abuse" is used throughout this book to refer to the physical and emotional harm done to women by their male mates, married or unmarried. While there have been a number of terms devised that would appear more inclusive (for example, spouse abuse, partner abuse, woman abuse), we think wife abuse best conveys the phenomenon our study focuses on. The word *wife* suggests not only the gender of the victims but also their perceived role in the relationship.

3. The comparison draws on other major empirical studies of battered women. The Stacey and Shupe (1983) sample (N = 542) of shelter women in the Dallas area from 1980–82 uses a shorter version of the questionnaire on which our study is based. The Pagelow (1981) study offers another sample of sheltered women (N = 350), in this case volunteers largely from California shelters and a Florida shelter. The Walker (1984) sample (N = 400) presents a quasi control of volunteer nonrandomized respondents from the Rocky Mountain region who were both in and out of shelters and more likely to not be in a battering relationship at the time of the interviews.

The Bowker study (1983) poses the other extreme in its sample of recruited formerly battered women (N = 146) who had been free of abuse for at least a year. This sample of Milwaukee women participated in a four-hour interview process. Bowker (1986) subsequently expanded this sample to a national sample (N = 1,000) recruited through magazine ads and surveyed through mailed questionnaires. The demographics and results of the national sample were comparable to the first.

The Bowker and Pagelow studies are the only ones that include specific correlations for helpseeking behavior. Unfortunately, the existing comparison groups do not have a complete set of matching variables. Also there is as yet no distinct control group of battered women who have not gone to a shelter.

4. The state spouse abuse survey (Teske and Parker 1983) sampled women with state driver's licenses (N = 2,000, with a response rate of 60.5 percent). Therefore, the respondents were of a much higher socioeconomic status, on average, than the shelter sample. This difference was reflected racially, as well: less than 9 percent of the sample was black and less than 9 percent was Hispanic. The sample from the statewide survey experienced less severe abuse as a group. Thirty percent (n = 359) of this sample had been victims of physical abuse sometime during their lifetime. Forty percent of the abused women in this sample had been punched, as opposed to 72 percent of the shelter sample, and only 8 percent had been abused with a knife or gun, as opposed to 30 percent of the shelter sample. A surprisingly small group sought shelter, but a substantial portion did separate from the batterer. Only 2 percent of the abused women had used shelter services in their lifetime, and 30 percent had contacted the police (as opposed to nearly 50 percent of the shelter women). However, in as many as one-half of the cases, the husband or abused woman moved out of the residence during the previous year, and 63 percent had divorced their batterer. This high percentage of separation without the aid of shelter may reflect the relative affluence of the survey sample and the mobility that affluence permitted. In any case, this evidence, even without the benefit of cross-tabulations, suggests that a substantial portion of the women not in shelter are actively asserting themselves by either seeking help or formulating a sort of self-help.

2
The Survivor Theory

Our assertion that battered women are active survivors raises a fundamental theoretical issue. It appears to contradict the prevailing characterization that battered women suffer from learned helplessness. According to learned helplessness, battered women tend to "give up" in the course of being abused; they suffer psychological paralysis and an underlying masochism that needs to be treated by specialized therapy. Our survivor hypothesis, on the other hand, suggests that women respond to abuse with helpseeking efforts that are largely unmet. What the women most need are the resources and social support that would enable them to become more independent and leave the batterer. (See table 2–1.)

In this chapter, we examine in more detail the theoretical basis for these two contrasting characterizations of battered women. First, the assumptions of learned helplessness are discussed. We consider also the experimental research underlying learned helplessness and its application to battered women. Second, we present the basis of a survivor theory with an overview of our survivor hypothesis, a summary of the supportive empirical research, and a redefinition of the symptoms of learned helplessness.

Finally, the implications of the alternative survivor theory are raised. There appears to be learned helplessness among the help sources designed to aid the battered women. The help sources need to be "treated," and the patriarchal assumptions that debilitate the available help sources need to be addressed.

Learned Helplessness

The Prevailing Characterization

The battered woman has been typically characterized as a helpless and passive victim. Lenore Walker's ground-breaking book, *The Battered Woman* (1979), noted that the battered woman becomes "psychologically paralyzed" as a result of learned helplessness. As animal experiments have demonstrated, there is a

Table 2–1
Comparison of Learned Helplessness and Survivor Hypothesis

Learned Helplessness

1. Severe abuse fosters a sense of helplessness in the victim. Abuse as a child and the neglect of help sources intensifies this helplessness. The battered woman is consequently severely victimized.
2. The victim experiences low self-esteem, self-blame, guilt, and depression. The only way to feel some sense of control over what is otherwise an unpredictable environment is to think that "if *I* change my ways, things will get better." But the abuse continues.
3. The victim eventually becomes psychologically paralyzed. She fails to seek help for herself and may even appear passive before the beatings. When she does contact a help source, she is very tentative about receiving help and is likely to return to the batterer despite advice or opportunity to leave.
4. This vulnerability and indecisiveness prolongs the violence and may contribute to its intensification. Some observers argue that this tendency may reflect an underlying masochism in the battered woman. The woman may feel that she deserves to be beaten and accepts it as a fulfillment of her expectations.
5. Battered women as victims need primarily psychological counseling to treat their low self-esteem, depression, and masochism. Cognitive therapy that addresses attributions of blame for the abuse may also be particularly effective in motivating the victim.

Survivor Hypothesis

1. Severe abuse prompts innovative coping strategies from battered women and efforts to seek help. Previous abuse and neglect by help sources lead women to try other help sources and strategies to lessen the abuse. The battered woman, in this light, is a "survivor."
2. The survivor may experience anxiety or uncertainty over the prospects of leaving the batterer. The lack of options, know-how, and finances raise fears about trying to escape the batterer. The battered woman may therefore attempt to change the batterer instead of attempting to leave.
3. The survivor actively seeks help from a variety of informal and formal help sources. There is most often inadequate or piecemeal helpgiving that leaves the woman little alternative but to return to the batterer. The helpseeking continues, however.
4. The failure of help sources to intervene in a comprehensive and decisive fashion allows abuse to continue and escalate. The inadequacy of help sources may be attributed to a kind of learned helplessness experienced in many community services. Service providers feel too overwhelmed and limited in their resources to be effective and therefore do not try as hard as they might.
5. Battered women as survivors of abuse need, most of all, access to resources that would enable them to escape the batterer. Community services need to be coordinated to assure the needed allocation of resources and integrated to assure long-term comprehensive intervention.

tendency to become submissive in the face of intermittent punishments or abuse. Similarly, the battered woman is immobilized amidst the uncertainty of when abuse will occur. She begins to feel that she has no control over her experience. No matter what she does, she "gets it." In the process, the victim begins to blame herself for the abuse. This self-blame implies some recourse or control over the otherwise unpredictable abuse. "If only I change myself, then the abuse will stop." Lenore Walker (1979:49–50) summarizes the victimization this way:

> In applying the learned helplessness concept to battered women, the process of how the battered woman becomes victimized grows clearer. Repeated batterings, like electrical shocks (in animal experiments), diminish the woman's

motivation to respond. She becomes passive. Secondly, her cognitive ability to perceive success is changed. She does not believe her response will result in a favorable outcome, whether or not it might. Next, having generalized her helplessness, the battered woman does not believe anything she does will alter any outcome, not just the specific situation that has occurred. She says, "No matter what I do, I have no influence." She cannot think of alternatives. She says, "I am incapable and too stupid to learn how to change things." Finally, her sense of emotional well-being becomes precarious. She is more prone to depression and anxiety.

Battered women, therefore, appear to need specialized counseling to address their debilitated psychological state. A number of clinical studies have, in fact, prescribed treatment for the battered woman's lack of self-esteem and fragmented identity (Rieker and Carmen 1986), feelings of loss and inadequacy (Turner and Shapiro 1986), or isolation and anxiety that is traced to abuse as a child (Weingourt 1985). Feminist critics, however, have strongly objected to the implication that battered women provoke or prolong abuse and generally require psychological counseling (Schechter 1982).

The Experimental Basis

The prevailing notion of learned helplessness is drawn from the extensive laboratory research of Martin Seligman of the University of Pennsylvania (Seligman and Maier 1967). During the late sixties, Dr. Seligman led a team of researchers experimenting with dogs in studies that would raise the ire of today's animal rights activists. The animals, after a series of intermittent electric shocks, eventually became immobilized. They would not escape from their cages even when an open route was provided for them. There is even evidence that this learned helplessness could immobilize a victim to the point of death.

The research was gradually extended to a variety of species and eventually to humans. In fact, Seligman's work was initially devoted to explaining America's most prevalent mental disorder: depression (see Seligman 1975). Since then, the notion of learned helplessness has gained a broad currency. Seligman alluded to prisoners of war, political prisoners, concentration camp detainees, and institutionalized patients as vulnerable to learned helplessness. Learned helplessness has also been used to explain the low motivation among some welfare recipients, the fatalism evident among many Third World peasants, and the persistent economic failure of some industrial towns (see Lanz 1972).

Explanations of Battered Women

It is not surprising, then, that the notion of learned helplessness has become a fixture in the domestic violence field as well. Battered women, as the theory goes, typically are conditioned to tolerate the abuse as a result of persistent and intermittent reinforcement from the batterer. The community lack of response to the abuse, and frequent accusation that the woman contributed to the abuse, further the helplessness. The cage door is shut, so to speak, and the women have no apparent way out.

Additionally, studies have suggested that learned helplessness may be rooted in childhood exposure to violence. Exposure to violence as a child may, in fact, predispose a woman to an abusive relationship as an adult (Bernard and Bernard 1983; Kalmuss 1984). She may grow up thinking that abuse is normal, or feel such shame and rejection that she expects and accepts the worst. The relationship between abuse as a child and as an adult may, however, be spurious or inevitable given the amount of violence in and around our homes (Dobash and Dobash 1979; Pagelow 1984; Walker 1984). Perhaps a more acceptable position is that the batterers appear to be "violence prone," and not battered women (Walker 1984).

Another popular explanation for what appears as learned helplessness is the "brainwashing" that a woman experiences in an abusive relationship as an adult. The batterer's manipulation and control of the woman has, in fact, been likened to the tactics used by brainwashers in prisoner-of-war camps. Eventually the captive is psychologically broken down to the point of relinquishing any sense of autonomy and complying to all the wishes of the captor.

Psychologists Donald Dutton and Susan Painter (1981) have similarly applied the theory of "traumatic bonding" to battered women. They point out that the abuse leaves the victim emotionally and physically drained and in desperate need of some human support or care. She is therefore likely to respond to the batterer's apologies and affection after the abuse. In this vulnerable state, she may sympathize and overidentify with the batterer, much as some prisoners of war or concentration camps have become sympathetic toward their guards. In essence, the trauma makes the woman prone to a kind of masochism.

Helplessness as Masochism

Although the initial application of learned helplessness to battered women was not intended to implicate masochism, it has been explicitly extended to do so. Several clinicians have viewed women's inclination to stay in violent relationships as evidence of their desire for abuse (see Kleckner 1978; Shainess 1979; Snell et al. 1964). These "experts" suggest that there is some emotional or existential exhilaration in being a victim. That is, women look for trouble and bring some of it on themselves. Some victims simply don't feel like they deserve any better and are not satisfied until that self-perception is fulfilled.

The legacy of Freud, in particular, has much of the psychology field still asserting that women are predisposed to masochism. As Barbara Ehrenreich and Deirdre English (1979) wrote in their book, *For Her Own Good: 150 Years of the Experts' Advice to Women*, the psychoanalytic view has shaped the medical and psychological treatment of women with mounting acceptance. In this view, women innately tolerate and even welcome more pain than men, in part because of their destiny to receive forceful penetration during sexual intercourse, as Helen Deutsch (1944) notes in her influential psychoanalytical work, *The Psychology of Women*. Also, women's aggressions are turned inward and expressed in self-blame and shame, because society limits their outward expression.

Natalie Shainess (1984), in *Sweet Suffering: Woman as Victim*, revises and extends the psychoanalytic notion of masochism to contemporary women. She insists that women contribute to their victimization by acting indecisive and vulnerable. She describes what she terms the "masochistic personality" of women who tend to seek out and exacerbate their abuse.

Dr. Shainess (1984:127) argues, in fact, that learned helplessness is really another term for masochism:

> Masochistic women DO do things that make them more vulnerable than they need to be. They DO send out messages signaling inadequacy, helplessness, and fear, which in a dangerous situation may make them more powerless than they need be. No one does women a favor by denying this. The term "masochim" has been in use for so long, both generally and professionally, that I think it is useless to try to eliminate it.

In Shainess's conception, however, masochism is learned developmentally and culturally, rather than predestined as the Freudians suggest. This may in part be related to growing up in abusive homes and thinking, as a result, that abuse is normal, or to internalizing the persistent subjugation and degradation of women in society at large. The masochism can be unlearned, therefore, by being more assertive and decisive in interpersonal relations. The popularity of books like *Women Who Love Too Much* appear to speak to this notion that women make themselves vulnerable and dependent and can solve this problem by simply being more assertive.

Reformulations of Helplessness

The learned helplessness theory has admittedly been critiqued and reformulated in recent years (see especially Abramson et al. 1978). Its earlier versions reflected the assumptions of behaviorist conditioning. Like the animals in Seligman's experiments, humans appeared to be "trained" into submission and learned helplessness. Their situation appeared to determine their behavior. In sum, learned helplessness was a conditioned reaction to the unpredictable punishments one received.

The advent of cognitive psychology has introduced the role of individual expectations and attributions in mediating learned helplessness (see Janoff–

Bulman and Frieze 1983). In this view, one's *perceptions* of the environment are what most influence one's reaction to it. If an individual perceives a series of punishments or failures as outside of his or her control, then learned helplessness is more likely.

Similarly, several qualitative studies of battered women have shown that their assumptions about their social environment contribute to their reactions to abuse (Frieze 1979; Mills 1985; Ferraro and Johnson 1983). However, rather than confirm learned helplessness, these studies actually open the door to alternative explanations. The women, rather than being passive recipients of the violence, appear instead as participants in the definition of the relationship and of themselves. If anything, the battered women *learn*, as the abuse escalates, that the self-blame associated with learned helplessness is inappropriate.

Interviews with self-identified battered women show that the women are more likely to blame themselves for the abuse after the first incident (Frieze 1980). Consequently they may attempt to change their behavior to please their batterers and avoid further abuse. As is usually the case, the violence recurs and escalates despite the women's efforts to please their batterers. They begin, therefore, to increasingly blame the batterer (that is, attribute the cause to him) and seek ways to change him. When these fail, the women then seek more decisive intervention and means to establish their own safety.

There is some suggestion, however, that there is a limit to this initiative. After repeated unsuccessful attempts to control the battering, some women may then begin to give up and lessen their helpseeking (Okum 1986). This resignation, after an intermediate phase of active helpseeking, differs from the conventional notion of learned helplessness in which there is a progression toward total brainwashing. (See table 2–2 for a summary of this attributional helpseeking progression.)

Another interview study (Mills 1985), with a small sample of shelter residents, suggests that the women experience a loss of self; for example, they mention feeling like a zombie, a robot, or simply numb amidst the violence. They begin to lose their "observing self" as well, in that they doubt and question their judgment and interpretation of events. However, the battered women continue to have "insights" about their relationship and their batterers' definition of the situation. They occasionally act on these insights by seeking verification of or response to them. The women also creatively and valiantly develop coping strategies intended to reduce the severity of the abuse. Eventually, with sufficient confirmation of the insights, they begin to define themselves as "survivors," —as individuals who are aware of their strength in enduring the abuse. They muster self-respect for that endurance and attempt to improve their situation.

This shift in perception begins to occur after any one of a variety of catalysts: a change in the level of violence, a change in resources, a change in the relationship, severe despair, a change in the visibility of violence, and external interventions that redefine the relationship. Any of these prompt a

Table 2–2
Attributional and Helpseeking Progression

First Incidents
The woman blames herself for the abuse. This is in part the result of the expectations of marriage in which she is to be a nurturer. The woman therefore attempts to change her own behavior and adequately please the batterer. The woman may attempt to get some advice from some informal help sources, such as family or friends. If she fails to get sufficient support and proper advice, she may begin to doubt her own judgment.

Recurring Abuse
The battered woman begins to realize that there is more to the abuse than her displeasing the batterer. She begins therefore to blame the batterer for some of the abuse and seeks to change him. She may call the police or contact a shelter. Her attempts fail and the abuse escalates. Her "insights" into the dynamics continue to grow, however.

Escalating Abuse
The battered woman eventually realizes that the batterer is not likely to change. She seeks more decisive intervention through legal assistance and explores ways to live separate from the batterer. If these efforts fail, the battered woman may continue in the abusive relationship and personally cope with the abuse as best she can. If the woman does receive appropriate support, she begins to accept herself as a "survivor" and continues the long process of helpseeking required to live safely on her own.

rejection of the previous rationalizations or denials of abuse, according to a qualitative study by Kathleen Ferraro and John Johnson (1983).

Not only are the women's perceptions seen as basic to their reaction, these perceptions also evolve and change. In fact, the tentative findings suggest that battered women are rational in their response. They hold to societal conceptions of their duty in a relationship until that conception is no longer plausible. The catalysts for change are not "treatment" of the symptoms of learned helplessness but rather a change in situational evidence or events that necessitates an adjustment in one's perceptions and attribution. As has been argued about other oppressed or victimized people, the women's "grievance" has to be confirmed (Davies 1971) and resources made available (Oberschall 1973) in order for them to become "mobilized."

Toward a Survivor Theory

The Survivor Hypothesis

The alternative characterization of battered women is that they are active survivors rather than helpless victims. (See table 2–1 for a comparison of the two characterizations.) As suggested above, battered women remain in abusive situations not because they have been passive but because they have tried to escape with no avail. We offer, therefore, a survivor hypothesis that contradicts the assumptions of learned helplessness: Battered women increase their helpseeking in the face of increased violence, rather than decrease helpseeking as learned helplessness would suggest. More specifically, we contend that helpseeking is likely to increase as wife abuse, child abuse, and the batterer's antisocial behavior (substance abuse, general violence, and arrests) increase. This help-seeking may be mediated, as current research suggests, by the resources available to the woman, her commitment to the relationship, the number of children she has, and the kinds of abuse she may have experienced as a child.

The fundamental assumption is, however, that woman seek assistance in proportion to the realization that they and their children are more and more in danger. They are attempting, in a very logical fashion, to assure themselves and their children protection and therefore survival. Their effort to survive transcends even fearsome danger, depression or guilt, and economic constraints. It supersedes the "giving up and giving in" which occurs according to learned helplessness. In this effort to survive, battered women are, in fact, heroically assertive and persistent.

Empirical Research

There are at least a few empirical studies that substantiate this hypothesis that battered women are survivors. The studies by Lee Bowker (1983), Mildred Pagelow (1981), and Lenore Walker (1984) indicate quantitatively that the helpseeking efforts of battered women are substantial.

Perhaps the most significant of these empirical works is Walker's *The Battered Women's Syndrome* (1984), designed to verify the author's original learned helplessness and "cycle of violence" theorization. Walker found, however, that the women in her Rocky Mountain sample were not necessarily beaten into submissiveness; rather, helpseeking increased as the positive reinforcements within the relationship decreased and the costs of the relationship in terms of abusiveness and injury increased.

As Walker (1984:27) illustrates:

> As the violence escalated, so did the probability that the battered women would seek help. While only 14 percent sought help after the first battering incident, 22 percent did after the second, 31 percent after one of the worst, and 49 percent sought help after the last incident. About one-quarter of the women left temporarily immediately after each battering incident, although these were not necessarily the same women each time.

Furthermore, the battered women in the Walker sample did not score significantly lower on psychological tests for the externalized control, weak self-esteem, or depression associated with learned helplessness than did a control group of women not in abusive relationships. In sum, the symptoms of learned helplessness did not appear to characterize or distinguish the battered women.

The Myth of Masochism

The implications of female masochism raised with learned helplessness have been similarly challenged. As the empirical studies suggest, battered women do not appear to be "victim prone." Women contribute to the violence only in the fact that they are female. As Paula Caplan (1985) in *The Myth of Female Masochism* forcefully argues, too often the feminine qualities of self-denial, trustfulness, nurturing, and friendliness are reinterpreted as naiveté and vulnerability.

Furthermore, it is highly debatable that assertiveness and carefulness in themselves can lessen one's vulnerability. Numerous studies have shown that male violence is for the most part indiscriminate and unpredictable. Gloria Steinem (1983) poignantly alludes to this in reevaluating the severely abused porno star, Linda Lovelace. She likens looking for some predisposition or inclination for abuse to asking, "What in your background led you to a concentration camp?"

The reinforcements for male violence against women, as feminists like Diana Russell (1984) in *Sexual Exploitation* emphatically declare, supersede women's efforts to resist or avoid abuse. There is a social system of patriarchy that denies women a way out. To be the autonomous person, which Shainess (1984) prescribes as an antidote to masochism, requires financial support, job training, dependable child care, adequate housing, and personal transportation that are not available to the majority of battered women—or women in general, for that matter.

The notion of female masochism focuses on deficiencies in the women and may be responsible for the research preoccupation with why women stay with their batterers. Much of the research on this matter has, however, demonstrated that women are reluctant to leave primarily because they can't (see Kalmuss and Straus 1982; Strube and Barbour 1983). They do not have a safe place to go, are not able to support themselves, or fear reprisals.

In light of the feminist challenge to female masochism, the more appropriate question may be "Why do so many men get away with woman battering?" When a man assaults another man or stranger outside the home, we ask, "Why did he do it?" The assumption is that there is something wrong with him, not the victim, that has to be addressed. But when a man assaults his wife or partner, the tendency is to focus first on why the victim doesn't have sense enough to avoid the violence.

The Female Survivor Instinct

How then do we explain the survivor tendency of battered women? Anthropologists have long argued that females have an instinctual tendency to attempt to preserve life through their nurturing and cooperative habits, whereas males are inclined toward aggression and destruction that might be seen as part of protecting one's own. According to the biological determinist view, these characteristics are rooted in the physiological differences that enable females to bear children and the more muscular male to hunt game for the family or fight to defend it. Sociologists, on the other hand, see the differences reinforced, if not generated, by the social roles ascribed to women as domestic servants and men as public servants. (See Tavris and Wade 1984 for a review of the research on this subject.)

Some modern feminists have redefined the biological determinism of the past in their rendition of social biology. They argue, rather impressively, that the woman's unique capacity for birthing and mothering has given women an appreciation for life that men can only emulate. Menstruation and other bodily changes, furthermore, link women with "nature" in ways that broaden their conceptions of the world. In other words, the female worldview is more in touch with life processes and reveres them more. It is consequently more global, inclusive, and harmonizing.

Feminist psychologists have asserted the moral superiority of this female reasoning process as well. Mainstream psychology, according to the feminists, has evaluated the female experience as deficient because it has assessed women with a male norm. Most notably, Carol Gilligan (1982), in her revision of developmental psychology *In A Different Voice*, identifies the female tendency to respond to moral issues with collaborative and accommodating solutions, as opposed to the more competitive and discriminating solutions of males. Women value most their personal relationships, rather than the instrumental ends that appear to preoccupy men in an "ends justify the means" mentality.

According to Gilligan, the feminine worldview is much more appropriate for the modern world than the masculine worldview that may have been better suited for a less delicate era of the past. The environmental and armament crises, for instance, warrant a more global, nurturing, and cooperative frame of mind.[1] The masculine worldview has, in fact, contributed to the battering of the weak and less fortunate and the rape of the land.

Self-transcendence in Helpseeking

These assertions about women survivors may reflect a more fundamental philosophical assumption about human nature in general. The survivor tendency we see in battered women is more than self-assertion, self-actualization, or self-determination. It may reflect what Frankl (1959) and others have referred to as "self-transcendence." An inner strength, yearn for dignity, desire for good, or will to live appears despite one's previous conditioning and present circumstances. Even in the midst of severe psychological impairment, such as depression, many battered women seek help, adapt, and push on. This is not to say that we should expect battered women, or other survivors of misfortune, to bounce back on their own. Rather, by receiving the proper supports, one's inner strength can be realized, resiliency demonstrated, and a new life made.

This process is one that must be supported by helpers rather than invoked by them. This is accomplished by what some call a reflexive approach; that is, helpers accentuate the potential for self-transcendence in others by display-ing it in themselves. The challenge is, therefore, for helpers to express resiliency, determination, and optimism, rather than succumb to the learned helplessness of so many bureaucratized help sources. As a result, so-called clients are more likely to discover and express their own resiliency. This approach is not some pollyanna or positive thinking. It is a matter of community building—that is, creating a place where positive role models promote mutual support.

Shelters have afforded one of the most promising experiments in this regard. Women and children, by virtue of their circumstances, are joined in a kind of intentional community where not only emotions and experience are shared but also the common tasks of daily life. The "muddling with the mundane" in the communal living arrangements of shelters—the negotiating and even haggling over food, shelter, and children—potentially teaches much in itself (Gondolf 1984). If managed effectively, shelter life may encourage women to assert themselves in new ways, clarify issues and fears, and collaborate with other women in need. In the process, the intimidating isolation that so many bat-tered women experience is broken and an internal fortitude released.

Redefining the Symptoms

This is not to deny the observations of shelter workers that some battered women do experience severe low self-esteem, guilt, self-blame, depression, vulnerability, and futility—all of which are identified with learned helplessness. Some battered women may even appear to act carelessly and provocatively at times, as the proponents of masochism argue. But cast in another light, these "symptoms" take on a different meaning, as well as a different proportion.

The so-called symptoms of learned helplessness may in fact be part of the adjustment to active helpseeking. They may represent traumatic shock from the abuse, a sense of commitment to the batterer, or separation anxiety amidst an unresponsive community. All of these are quite natural and healthy responses but not entirely acceptable ones in a patriarchal (or male-dominated) society that values cool detachment. Not to respond with some doubts, anxiety, or depression would suggest emotional superficiality and denial of the real dif-ficulties faced in helpseeking.

First, the symptoms of learned helplessness may be a temporary manifesta-tion of *traumatic shock*. Many of the women arriving at shelters have suffered severe physical abuse equivalent to what one might experience in a severe auto accident. What appears as physical unresponsiveness or psychological depres-sion may therefore be more an effort of the body and mind to heal themselves. The women, rather than being passive and withdrawn personalities, are going through a necessary healing process. They need not so much psychotherapy as time and space to recuperate.

Second, the symptoms may reflect an effort by battered women to *save the relationship*. Seeking help represents, in some sense, an admission of failure to fulfill the traditional female role of nurturing and domesticity. It appears to some women, too, as a breach of the marriage vow to love and honor one's spouse. As several of the interview studies show (Ferraro and Johnson 1983; Mills 1985), battered women do initially blame themselves for not being nurturing, supportive, or loving enough to make the marriage work. It is important, however, to distinguish this initial sense of failure from the sense of an uncontrollable universe which underlies learned helplessness (Abramson et al. 1978).

Third, the depression and guilt in some shelter women (Mitchell and Hodson 1983) may be an expression of *separation anxiety* that understandably accompanies leaving the batterer. The women face tremendous uncertainty in separating even temporarily from the batterer. They fear reprisals for leaving, loss of custody of the children, and losing their home and financial support. The unknown of trying to survive on one's own can be as frightening as returning to a violent man. The prospects of obtaining employment sufficient to support oneself and children are minimal for most shelter women, especially considering their lack of previous experience and education. This coupled with the feminization of poverty in contemporary America (Sidel 1986) makes a return to the batterer the lesser of the two evils. At least there is a faint hope that the batterer will change, whereas the prospects for change in the larger community seem less favorable.

Treating the Helpers

Helplessness among Helpers

In sum, many battered women make contact with a variety of helping sources in response to their abuse. As the abuse becomes more severe and the batterer more apparently beyond change, the diversity of the woman's contacts actually increases. We argue that this represents a survivor tendency of strength and resiliency. Depression, guilt, and shame may accompany a battered woman, but these should not be used to characterize battered women in general or to label them as victims of learned helplessness.

The prevailing notion of learned helplessness may, in fact, be misleading. Learned helplessness suggests that it is the woman who needs to be diagnosed and treated. Admittedly, some women do need tremendous emotional support and mental health care in the wake of devastating abuse. However, we believe that there is a more important side to consider: the insufficient response of community help sources.

If learned helplessness is a valid conception, it is ironically prevalent in the system of helping sources. It is more likely that agency personnel suffer from insufficient resources, options, or authority to make a difference, and therefore are reluctant to take decisive action (Bass and Rice 1979; McEvoy et al. 1983; McShane 1979). Too often, community services respond singularly to a problem rather than in some coordinated and mutually reinforcing fashion. This too cannot help but cause a sense of diffusion and duplication. There remains, furthermore, a reductionism that would treat abuse as a symptom of some other disorder or accident (Adams 1986; Kurz 1987). In fact, emergency room staff have been accused of "cooling out" the abused woman with tranquilizer medications that actually reduce the woman's ability to respond effectively to her abuse (Stark et al. 1979; Kurz 1987).

It is our community systems of care and intervention that need treatment. Granted, the battered woman's contact with the clergy, human services, police, and legal assistance may at times be tentative. But the women meet an equally tentative response from the helpers. Malpractice suits, no-risk clauses, privatization of services, severe funding cutbacks, and a laissez-faire public attitude have brought reluctance rather than initiative to the helping professions.

Certainly more than new community programs are needed to counteract the impact of this state of affairs. Many of the social problems we face today—pockets of severe unemployment, generations of poverty among minority groups, increased immigration and opposing discrimination—require governmental leadership, if not activism, and perhaps some personal intrusions.

"Getting Tough"

We have seen recently a promising "get tough" trend with drug use and drunk driving. However expedient and superficial, the government-supported intervention and intrusion in these areas are decisive and apparently are having some impact. Domestic violence will require no less. The boundaries of family privacy will have to be crossed, not only to assure the safety of women and children but also to prevent the long-term side effects of domestic violence—impoverished, single-parent households; emotionally hampered children; and generational recurrence of violence. The cost to society for these latter problems is simply too great to tolerate.

This call to action is not meant to be an alarmist outburst overstepping reasoned restraints. What is needed is basically a better use and deployment of the existing services and interventions available in our respective communities. Community services need to be coordinated and integrated in a fashion that brings a decisive and comprehensive response to abuse. Essentially, a woman's contact with one helping source should be sufficient to call forth the response of the entire helping system. The helpers within the system, of course, need more than just a widened and reinforced "dragnet" in order to accomplish this. They need to become more acutely aware of the survivor character of battered women and of their own learned helpnessness. As a result of self-examination and restructuring within the helping professions, not only will battered women be better served, but the prospects of their feeling helpless will also be eliminated.

Addressing Patriarchal Assumptions

There is a temptation to leave the survivor critique of community services at this practical level. That is, there are deficiencies in our help sources that need to be remediated to better support the helpseeking efforts of battered women. But this critique fails to expose the underlying assumptions that contribute to the preoccupation with learned helplessness in the first place and to the breakdown of help sources in the second.

According to feminist analysis, patriarchy—a system of male dominance—underlies much of the tendency to characterize women as deficient and to respond insufficiently. But it emerges in the helpseeking of battered women not so much as a conscious conspiracy of males against females but as a style of thought and interaction that is "masculine" in its deference to hierarchy, expertise, technique, and individualism. This approach has emphasized a pathological analysis of problems, a medical model of treatment, and privitization of family life.

The first patriarchal assumption rooted deep in our society is that problems are caused by some *individual pathology*. Our social policies tend to address deviance and dysfunction in individuals or families rather than in the structures of society as a whole. In fact, social policy is more often used to preserve that social structure rather than change it. The result is that individuals are to be restrained or managed for the social well-being. Our social science must therefore identify what is "wrong" with individuals and find ways to "fix" them or bring them back to the norm. Allocating resources to women in a way that would increase their social status or power is therefore resisted.

A second patriarchal assumption is that *the medical model* of professional expertise is the most appropriate form of treatment. The medical model has loosely been characterized as experts treating the problem "within" the person. That is, there is some dysfunction in the body or mind that is responsible for socially deviant acts. This orientation has given rise to an abundance of clinical psychologies that look for the root of our problems in the dysfunction of our thought processes and seek to right them through expert persuasion. Most of these "treatments" are technique-based; they impersonalize the helping process by slighting the emotional nurturing, mutual self-disclosure, and long-term commitment that are so fundamental to the feminine perspective.

A third patriarchal assumption at odds with the survivor notion is the continued *privatization of family life*. At a time of tremendous social transition and dislocation, there is a tendency to allow and expect families to fend for themselves in the name of autonomy. While families or individual family members may receive "treatment," it is increasingly difficult to obtain adequate housing, child care, income assistance, and meaningful employment. This is especially the case for single women attempting to enter the work force while caring for children. The "masculinized" systems have been short particularly on credit, alimony, and child support for single-parent women whose standard of living tends to collapse after divorce or separation.

The point is this: In order to more substantially and realistically address social problems on the order of wife abuse, we ultimately need to relax our underlying masculine assumptions about "the way it spozed to be." We must dare to confront the demands of social reform from a more feminine point of view. That doesn't necessarily connote some radical overturning or autocratic governmental scheme. It is more likely to come, as many realignments have come throughout history, in a social "awakening" and realignment of values. Some might argue that it could be the outgrowth of a continued "feminization of America" (Lenz and Myerhoff 1985) in which women and feminine values continue to play a fuller role in society.

Note

1. There is of course some qualification that might be made to this female survivor explanation. It is plausible that the helpseeking we observed is exceptional rather than gender-based. The shelter women may be a group of resilient personalities. That is, they may be individuals who defied the learned helplessness and underlying masochism of the majority of battered women to obtain help. One noted longitudinal study of resilient children shows how family circumstances contributed to the children's latter adaptability, despite debilitating poverty that would have them at risk of learned helplessness and social pathology (Werner and Smith 1982). The presence of surrogate parents (extended social support while growing up) was associated with resiliency in the adults. The battered women in shelters could be similar individuals. However, our preliminary evidence suggests that a substantial portion of the battered women experienced abuse as a child, rather than the kinds of social encouragement that were found in the childhood of the resilient individuals.

The study of exceptional resiliency nonetheless poses some principles that may lend support to our gender-based conception of the survival instinct. The resilient individuals were in moderately large families where they were expected to help take care of brothers and sisters, as well as cooperate in some selfless way for the benefit and survival of the family as a whole. The shelter women have similarly had to exercise tremendous nurturing and selflessness in their adult families in order to overcompensate for their batterers' abuse of them and their children. They need to survive themselves in order to take care of their children. Consequently, they as women must attempt to survive.

3
A Causal Model of Helpseeking

I n this chapter we present empirical evidence supporting our survivor hypothesis. After considering the findings of other studies, we summarize the help sources contacted by our Texas sample of shelter women. Then, a causal model of helpseeking is constructed using structural equation analysis. This model shows increased helpseeking in response to more dangerous abuse, as our survivor hypothesis suggests. The chapter concludes with the implications of this model for shelter programs and other community services.

Research on Battered Women's Helpseeking

Previous Studies

There have been only a few empirical studies that consider the helpseeking behavior of battered women. Two prominent studies of battered women that touch on the issue of helpseeking are Mildred Pagelow's (1981) *Woman-Battering* and Bowker's (1983) *Beating Wife Beating*. Pagelow (1981) examined the factors related to staying in an abusive relationship using a volunteer sample of shelter women (N = 350). Her findings suggest that a woman's traditional values, limited resources, and isolation from institutional assistance are at least mildly associated with remaining longer in an abusive relationship. In other words, social factors should be more conspicuous in the description of battered women's behavior.

Bowker's (1983) *Beating Wife Beating* interviewed formerly battered women (N = 146) recruited through newspaper advertisements and social services for their appraisal of various help sources. His results demonstrated that these formerly battered women had persistently sought a wide range of help and managed to end their abuse. In fact, the more intensified and prolonged the abuse of these women, the greater the variety and extent of their helpseeking.

Besides seeking help, some battered women may physically attack their batterers in an attempt to defend themselves or retaliate (Saunders 1986). Some physical retaliation was used by the Bowker sample after 29 percent of the battering incidents. About one-quarter of the women in the Walker (1984) sample pushed or shoved the batterer, and one-fifth clawed or scratched him during the worst incident. The life-threatening behavior toward the batterer, however, was minimal.

The previous studies that consider helpseeking substantiate the fact that a large portion of battered women have contacted various forms of informal and formal help sources. One-half to two-thirds of both the Pagelow and Bowker samples had previously contacted the police. About half of the women had contacted family members. The women's own relatives were more likely to be asked for help in connection with battering than any other help sources, except the police. Our findings conform to these tendencies.

Specific Findings

The findings of several studies document further that battered women have been in contact with a wide variety of help sources. The Pagelow study of shelter women showed that, sometime during the course of the relationship, 55 percent of the women contacted the police, as compared with 44 percent who contacted legal agents, 28 percent who contacted psychiatrists or psychologists, 22 percent who contacted the clergy, and 15 percent who contacted marriage counselors. The Bowker (1983) study considered the helpseeking after the last battering incident and found the following: Family members were contacted in 43 percent of the cases, friends in 52 percent, shelter services 29 percent, police 34 percent, social services 43 percent, legal agents 49 percent, clergy 15 percent, and women's groups 36 percent.

Frieze et al. (1980), in their sample of battered women in Pittsburgh (N = 150), had comparable results: Relatives were approached in 55 percent of the cases, as compared to 52 percent who contacted friends, 43 percent who contacted social services, 42 percent who contacted therapists, and 39 percent who sought out clergy. Nearly two-thirds had contacted the police and one-half had filed legal charges at some time during the relationship.

Shulman (1979), identifying battered women through a random sample of Kentucky wives, found less formal helpseeking. Sixty-one percent of those who had been battered discussed the abuse with a family member and 49 percent with a friend. Clergy were contacted by only 14 percent of the women, and agency workers or therapists by only 19 percent. This lower amount of helpseeking is in part a reflection of the fact that a substantial portion of Kentucky battered women had only experienced one or two incidents of abuse.

Amidst this extensive and diverse helpseeking, the widespread use of learned helplessness to explain the behavior of battered women may be another "woozle"—that is, a notion accepted as basic truth but based on common usage rather than empirical fact (Schrumm et al. 1982). The question remains, however, whether an alternative characterization of battered women can be empirically constructed—one that highlights an increase in helpseeking, rather than a decrease, in response to more severe abuse. We attempt below to develop an empirical model of the survivor theory using a structural equation analysis (LISREL). We begin, however, with an overview of the helpseeking behavior of the Texas shelter women.

The Helpseeking of the Texas Women

Measuring Helpseeking

The principal helpseeking variable used in our study is the women's "previous helpseeking." This is indicated in the respondent's answer to the question: "In general, immediately after abusive incidents, what have you done?" Thirteen categories of response to the abuse were offered: attempted suicide, covered up for the batterer, threatened the batterer or acted violent toward him, left home for a while, called a family member, called a friend, called a minister or other clergy, called a social service agency, called a shelter or a lawyer, visited a social service agency, called the police, previously visited a shelter, took legal action. As shown in table 3–1, these responses may be grouped within the typology developed by Bowker (1983): (1) personal strategies that include coping efforts that rely on the women's own resources, such as attempting suicide or threatening the batterer; (2) informal help sources that include advice or assistance drawn from relatives, friends, or clergy; and (3) formal help sources that are comprised of the social services and law enforcement.

We sorted the women's responses to abuse in a variety of ways in order to measure the level of helpseeking. For one, we considered the "positive efforts" as eleven of the thirteen responses that represented some positive assertion on the women's part. The "attempted suicide" and "covered up for the batterer" categories were therefore excluded from this measure. In terms of "positive efforts," the Texas women had made an average of five different kinds of efforts to stop the abuse (out of a possible eleven) prior to coming to the shelter.

It should be noted that these helpseeking responses do not account for any medical attention sought for the injuries incurred in the abuse, the visit to the shelter that brought the women into our sample, nor the helpseeking done since entering the shelter. (The latter helpseeking is discussed in chapter 6.) If we include, with the other helpseeking efforts, the professional treatment for injuries (obtained from counselors, doctors, emergency rooms, or hospitalization), the average number of helpseeking sources increases to six. As mentioned in chapter 1, 42 percent of the women sought hospital care for

Table 3–1
Frequencies for Previous Helpseeking

Category of Response	Responses (%)	Cases (%)
Personal Strategies		
Attempted suicide	3	14
Covered up for batterer	10	46
Threatened batterer[a]	8	35
Left home[a]	16	71
Informal Help Sources		
Called family[a, b]	10	47
Called friend[a, b]	10	47
Called minister[a, b]	4	17
Formal Help Sources (called)		
Called social service agency[a, b]	4	19
Called shelter or lawyer[a, b]	14	64
Called police[a, b]	12	54
Formal Help Sources (visited)		
Visited social service agency[a, b]	2	11
Visited shelter[a, b]	3	14
Took legal action[a, b]	4	19

[a]Helpseeking positive efforts (average = 4.8)
[b]Helpseeking contacts (formal and informal help sources) (average = 2.9)

their injuries. The addition of the current shelter contact raises the average overall to seven kinds of helpseeking efforts.

Second, we considered the previous helpseeking contacts made with only formal and informal help sources; all the personal strategies, including leaving home or threatening the batterer, were excluded. By this measure, the women contacted (called or visited) an average of three different sources out of nine. They had contacted on average two different sources of formal help after abusive incidents.

We might deduce from these measures alone that the shelter women have made assertive attempts to do something about their abuse. They have contacted a variety of formal as well as informal sources where one would expect to gain substantial help.

Kinds of Helpseeking

A look at the proportion of women who made each kind of response offers further insight into the helpseeking pattern. It appears that the majority of women made extremely assertive efforts to stop the abuse. The majority of the Texas women (71 percent) had previously left home before becoming shelter residents, as in the Bowker (1983) sample of women who had stopped the abuse (75 percent). In 63 percent of the cases, the women had contacted the shelter or a lawyer; and over half (53 percent) had called the police at least once (45 percent in the Stacey and Shupe sample). A substantial portion of women had also taken legal action against the batterers (see table 3–1).

Interestingly, the least-mentioned responses were visiting a social service agency (11 percent) or visiting a shelter (14 percent). The formerly battered women in the Bowker study found the shelters to be the "most helpful" and the clergy to be the "least helpful" (only 17 percent of our sample contacted the clergy).

Limitations

The measure for previous helpseeking has, of course, some limitations, but it remains instructive, in our estimation. "Previous helpseeking" merely suggests the *diversity* of helping sources contacted by a woman. It does not account for the number of contacts to any one helping source, the duration of the contact, the kind of assistance received, nor the effectiveness of the assistance.

Bowker's (1983) evaluative study did make some accounting for these aspects of helpseeking. The women in Bowker's sample received, on average, from six to eight instances of help per incident of abuse from informal sources such as family, friends, and neighbors, and they received from eight to nineteen instances from formal sources of help such as social services, lawyers, clergy, and women's groups. Extrapolating from these findings, we might expect that our Texas women made frequent contacts to the sources they indicated calling or visiting.

If we take a conservative average of eight instances of assistance per help source contacted and multiply that by the three average number of help sources contacted by our sample, we would have a minimum of twenty-four efforts of helpseeking per client. This approximation, moreover, does not account for the multiple battering incidents received by our sample, which would push the calculation even higher.

Bowker's (1983) study also considered the effectiveness of each help source. His findings in this regard are summarized as follows (Bowker and Maurer 1985:6):

> Battered women's shelters were more likely to be rated as very effective than any other formal source of help. Forty-four percent of shelter users rate their shelter experience as very effective in helping them to decrease or end the violence. Comparable ratings for other professional groups were: 30 percent for lawyers, 27 percent for women's groups, 23 percent for district attorneys, 20 percent for social service or counseling agencies, 19 percent for the police, 12 percent for the clergy, and 8 percent for physicians and nurses. Shelters were less likely than any other formal help source except the clergy and women's groups to be associated with increased violence.

The Bowker study noted, moreover, that a diversity of contacts was associated with ending the violence—not so much any one help source or the frequency of contacts overall. This would suggest that our helpseeking measure accounting for the diversity of efforts or contacts would be a meaningful measure in its own right. It may be the best indicator of the battered women's movement toward ending the abuse.

Constructing a Survivor Model

Proposed Model

We next attempted to construct a causal model that would explain this high level of helpseeking (see figure 3–1 for the proposed "survivor" model). As suggested by our survivor hypothesis, we expected that an increase in helpseeking was related to an increase in abuse (that is, there would be a "positive" association between the two variables). Several other factors may also contribute to the helpseeking, according to current research. One, the victim's income, as an indicator of economic independence, is likely to increase her helpseeking, or be positively associated (Kalmuss and Straus 1982; Strube and Barbour 1983). Two, a larger number of children is likely to be associated with more severe child abuse, as studies of child abuse indicate (Finkelhor 1984). Three, the batterer's antisocial behavior (substance abuse, general violence, and arrests) may be positively associated with more severe wife abuse (Fagan et al. 1983; Gondolf 1987) and more helpseeking (Bowker 1983; Frieze 1979; Pagelow 1981; Walker 1984).

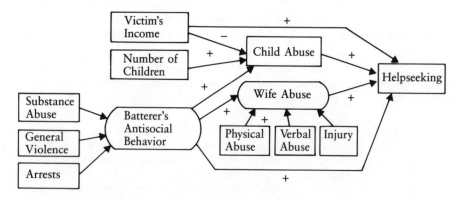

Notes: + = positive association—both variables increase.
       − = negative association—one variable increases, while the other decreases.

Figure 3–1. Proposed "Survivor" Model to be Tested

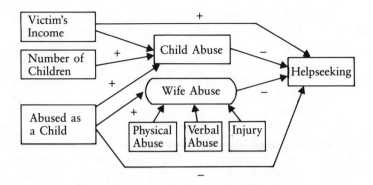

Notes: + = positive association—both variables increase.
      − = negative association—one variable increases, while the other decreases.

Figure 3–2. Prevailing "Learned Helplessness" Model

In essence, the helpseeking is a response to the batterer's violences and the woman's independence. This proposed survivor model contrasts, therefore, with the model suggested by the prevailing learned helplessness theory in two fundamental relationships (see figure 3–2). First, in the learned helplessness model, helpseeking would decrease with an increase in wife abuse or child abuse, or be negatively associated. Second, the abuse experienced as a child would predispose women to accept more abuse (positive association) and seek less help (negative association).

The variables selected from the Texas data base for a causal analysis of the helpseeking have some empirical basis for their inclusion. In an exploratory analysis of a variety of primary background, abuse, and helpseeking variables, these variables showed moderate bivariate correlations in the pattern suggested in the model (Gondolf et al. in press). This exploratory analysis, following the method of analysis employed by both Bowker (1983) and pagelow (1981), also identified a potentially influential variable that was not considered in our initial model, that is, "the batterer's response to abuse."

The Variables

The variables used in the causal model consist of observed variables, developed directly from the questionnaire, and latent variables, which are hypothetical constructs derived from a combination of observed variables. The *background variables* used in the initial model include two observed variables—the "victim's income" and "number of children"—and one latent variable—the "batterer's antisocial behavior." The latent variable is composed of three observed variables: the batterer's "substance abuse," "general violence," and "arrests." "Substance abuse" was calculated by combining the responses to three "yes–no" questions on both drug and alcohol abuse (for a total of six questions). The general violence and arrest variables are computed value scores. The measure for general violence is derived from six ranked categories of violences. The arrest variable was computed from nine different kinds of the batterer's arrests. (See appendix for further discussion of variable construction.)

An observed variable used in a revised model for no-arrest cases is the "batterer's response" to abuse. This variable represents the total number of different responses (nine possible) to the question, "How did the batterer generally respond to the abuse?" The higher totals reflect a greater inconsistency in the batterer's response, as well as a preponderance of negative reactions.

The *abuse variables* include the latent variable "wife abuse," which combines "verbal abuse," "physical abuse," "frequency of abuse," and "injury" from wife abuse, and an observed variable for the severity and frequency of "child abuse." The variables for verbal and physical abuse were the weighted scores computed from multiple-response questions (see chapter 1). The six ranked categories for verbal abuse ranged from "personal insult" to "threaten to harm children," and the ten categories for physical abuse ranged from "threw things at you" to "used weapon against you," conforming to the Conflict Tactics scale (Straus et al. 1980). Similarly, a weighted score was derived for injury from the abuse.

"Frequency of wife abuse" and "frequency of child abuse" were measured with an ordinal scale of incidents during the past six months. The frequency response level was, in turn, multiplied by the value score of the abuse (wife's physical abuse or child abuse) to account for the frequency of abuse in the wife abuse and child abuse scores.[1]

The *helpseeking variable* used in the analysis is the total number of different helpseeking "positive efforts" (eleven possible) made prior to coming to the shelter (see table 3–1).

The Model Analysis

The relationship among the variables was analyzed with the Linear Structural Relations Program (LISREL–VI) developed by Joreskog and Sorbom (1986).[2] As is customary with LISREL hypothesis testing, a measurement model and structural equation model were constructed. Two revised models (a learned helplessness model and a no-arrest model) were also tested with LISREL.

The measurement model for the survivor hypothesis (specifying the relationships of observed measures to latent variables) established wife abuse (a latent variable) as a construct of physical abuse, verbal abuse, and injury (observed variables), and antisocial behavior (latent) as a construct of substance abuse, general violence, and arrests (observed). Victim's income, number of children, child abuse, and helpseeking were incorporated into the model as measured.

The causal model links, first, the independent variable to the dependent variables consistent with the proposed survivor model depicted in figure 3–1: the victim's income to child abuse and helpseeking, number of children to child abuse; and antisocial behavior to child abuse, wife abuse, and helpseeking. Second, the dependent variables were linked among themselves as follows: child abuse, and wife abuse to helpseeking. As mentioned above, *the model essentially shows helpseeking as the outcome of the victim's income, antisocial behavior, child abuse, and wife abuse.*

Revised Model Tests

The prevailing learned helplessness model was tested by substituting "abuse as a child" for "batterer's antisocial behavior," as presented in figure 3–2. The "abuse as child" variable was constructed by adding the total number of kinds of abuse witnessed as child (that is, physical abuse between parents, alcohol abuse by parents, physical abuse of client by parents). This variable was introduced into the model as an independent variable and linked to child abuse, wife abuse, and helpseeking.

The survivor model was also revised to test the survivor hypothesis with no-arrest men. Since the initial findings showed antisocial behavior to be such an influential variable, it was unclear whether the survivor model held for less antisocial men. Therefore, the batterer's response variable was substituted for the antisocial variable and analyzed with a subgroup of cases with no arrests (and no violence to nonfamily members). The no-arrest cases comprised 43 percent of the total shelter sample. The revised model was also applied to a subgroup of serious arrest cases, as was a model with both antisocial and batterer response as independent variables.

The Model Findings

The initial survivor model, by all indications, appears to be an especially good one. The goodness-of-fit measures overall indicate that the model is suitable representation of the data.[3] The adjusted goodness-of-fit (AGFI), for instance, is .950 (unadjusted .986). The total coefficient of determination for y-variables is .934 and for the x-variables is .998, indicating the measurement model is strong. The coefficient of determination for the structural equation (CD–SE) at .729 confirms that the so-called inner model is reliable.

The standardized coefficients of the effects substantiate the hypothesis, for the most part (see figure 3–3). Helpseeking is shown to be positively related especially to antisocial behavior (.567), but only slightly related to the victim's

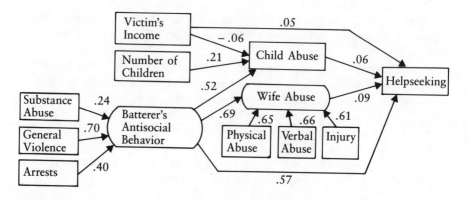

Notes: Coefficient of determination (for the structural equation) = .729. Adjusted goodness-of-fit index = .950. Root means square residual = .041.

Figure 3–3. "Survivor" Model with Standardized Coefficients (LISREL)

income (.047) and wife abuse (.085). It is only slightly related to child abuse (–.056), and in a negative direction.[4] Furthermore, the severity of child abuse has a negligible increase with higher income (.062), a modest increase with more children (.214), and a substantial increase with antisocial men (.522). The severity of wife abuse is also strongly influenced by the batterer's antisocial behavior (.693).[5]

The results for the revised models are as follows: One, the model for the no-arrest cases (n = 1,400) is comparable to the original survivor model, as indicated in figure 3–4 (AGFI = .847). The batterer's response variable, therefore, appears to be an equivalent substitute for antisocial behavior in cases where the batterer has never been arrested. If women do not have criminality to indicate the batterer's dangerousness, they are influenced by the batterer's response to them after the abuse.

Two, the learned helplessness model with previous abuse would not converge. Also, the previous abuse variable when inserted into the survivor model showed no significant effects, as other shelter studies have shown (Okum 1986; Pagelow 1984). This suggests that previous abuse does not predispose women to passive victimization.

Four, a trimmed version of the initial survivor model that deleted the link from the batterer's antisocial behavior to helpseeking was equivalent to the initial model (AGFI = .941; RMSR = .048), except that the coefficient from wife abuse to helpseeking increased dramatically. This trimmed version suggests that severe wife abuse accompanied by antisocial behavior increases helpseeking, while the severity of wife abuse in itself does not substantially influence helpseeking.

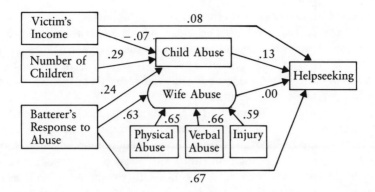

Notes: Coefficient of determination (for structural equation) = .729. Adjusted goodness-of-fit index = .847. Root means square residual = .025.

Figure 3–4. Revised "Survivor" Model for Nonarrest Cases (LISREL)

Summary and Implications

Summary

The survivor model developed here suggests that battered women do in fact respond to more severe abuse with increased helpseeking. It does not appear, however, that the helpseeking is a direct response to increased abuse by itself, but rather increases in the context of other batterer behavior. The helpseeking is apparently an effort to gain safety from generally dangerous men.

More specifically, the model indicates that the range of help sources contacted by the women increases as the batterer's antisocial behavior increases—or, in the case of no-arrested men, as the batterer's negative responses to the abuse increase. The more antisocial the batterer, the more severe his abuse and therefore, we might assume, the more apparent the danger.[6]

These findings lend support especially to the notion that battered women are more likely to leave a relationship when it is clear that the batterer is not going to change or that the batterer is a generally dangerous person (Frieze 1979). At that point, the woman's rationalizations for the abuse are less likely to suffice (Ferraro and Johnson 1983).

Implications

As we argue in chapter 2, this survivor model implies more of a "system failure" than a failure on the part of the battered woman. The helping sources appear to have failed to respond effectively to abuse on at least two counts. One, battered women have contacted a variety of helping sources in response to their dangerous situation, yet the helping services have apparently not been able to stop the abuse or assure safety. Two, the model suggests that the antisocial batterers have been elusive or unresponsive to the interventions designed to address such behavior (see Gondolf 1987). It is safe to assume that the extreme levels of substance abuse, general violence, or arrests by themselves would have warranted some decisive intervention.[7]

The survivor model, in this light, has several implications for shelter programs. It verifies that severely abused women have extensively sought help. They have a "drive to survive" that must be acknowledged, reinforced, and honored. However, many of these women appear to "fall through the cracks"; therefore, shelters need to intensify their advocacy role. Other community services need to be taught to effectively detect and aid battered women, as has long been argued (Borkowski et al. 1983). Conducting this sort of community education, however, is often at odds with the urgent demands of women in crisis, especially considering the limited resources of most shelters.

Conversely, the tendency to psychologize the abuse (Davis 1986; Johnson 1981) with psychotherapies for battered women may slight the survivor nature of the clients. The implication from the model is that the way to activate battered women to seek help and address their situation is to heighten the awareness of their batterers' antisocial nature and general incorrigibility, as Okum (1986) argues at the conclusion of his study of Michigan shelter women. Rather than treat the symptoms of learned helplessness in victims, we need to help them better appraise dangerousness and intervene more decisively with antisocial men.

Notes

1. An alternate variable for these value scores was also calculated. The total number of categories mentioned was computed for physical abuse, verbal abuse, arrests, and violence. These totals (without multiplying child and wife abuse by frequency) were inserted into the model in place of the value scores and analyzed with the LISREL procedures outlined below. The outcome was comparable to the model computed from value scores; the determination coefficient for the structural equation is .745, and the AGFI is .930.

2. This sort of analysis is superior to the bivariate correlations and limited regression analysis used in the Bowker (1983), Pagelow (1981), and Walker (1984) studies in three important ways. One, it accounts for the multivariate interaction effects, as a standard regression analysis does. Two, it controls for measurement errors in observed variables, which standard regression analysis is not able to do, and allows the construction of latent indices that are composites of observed variables. This is especially useful given the interrelated nature of many of the variables in this field and the need for more complex indicators, particularly for abuse. Three, this analysis examines the network of relations among dependent variables, as well as between independent and

dependent variables. The model in this way is better able to approximate the web of interrelationships that comprise social reality.

3. The model was derived from a correlation matrix of the ten variables (n = 925) using an unweighted least squares method (ULS). (This is the most appropriate procedure for a model with some ordinal or ordered categorical variables and some not normal in distribution. This procedure does not, however, compute standard errors and T-values like the maximum likelihood estimate (MLE) approach.)

The initial analyses suggested that victim's income should be linked (freed) to child abuse and that the error matrix for the independent observed variables (Theta Delta) should be freed between substance abuse and arrests. The latter is no doubt a reflection of substance abuse variables being computed with arrests for drunken driving or drug possession. These adjustments were made, along with starting victim's income at 0.9 because it was considered the most accurate measure in the model.

The chi-square is not reported since it is considered to be misleading with large sample sizes and not to be used as a test statistic in this form of analysis. The root means square residual (RMSR), used primarily for comparisons among models, is a relatively small value (.049), which further suggests a good fit.

4. This negative relationship may be a reflection of the limited mobility related especially to young and larger numbers of children.

5. Two minor trouble spots in the model should be noted. One, the Q-plot of the normalized residuals showed a slope of slightly less than one, an indication that the residuals are bordering on acceptable. This reflects, no doubt, the lack of true normality in a few of the constructed variables. The most extreme residuals are from the variables for substance abuse (2.58) and arrests (2.81). The normality of both these variables is distorted by the large number in the no-alcohol-abuse or no-arrests category (coded 0), and their reliability is affected by their somewhat arbitrary construction.

Replications of the model with a smaller sample (n = 525) and larger (n = 1,500) showed comparable results. For instance, the coefficient for the structural equation of the smaller sample is (.703) and the AGFI is .934; the maximum residual is only 2.31. The model, therefore, appears to be relatively stable.

6. It should be noted that racial and economic status do not differentiate the men in a statistically significant way. In other words, the more antisocial men are not more likely to be the poorer or minority men. (See Gondolf 1987b.)

7. This also might shed some light on a related issue of increasing attention: battered women who kill their husbands (Browne 1987). If, as the model suggests, women with severely dangerous men are extensively seeking help and not receiving it, and they face men who have been unrestrained for their antisocial behavior, much of which goes beyond the family, these unaided women may feel that they have no other recourse than to take matters into their own hands. The question then becomes: What is it about our society that tolerates not only wife abuse but the extremes of male antisocial behavior in general?

4
Differences among Shelter Women

O ur Texas sample is distinguished by a large portion of black and Hispanic women and by an emerging group of nonresident shelter women. Fifty-seven percent of the Texas shelter women are white, 15 percent are black, and 29 percent are Hispanic; nearly a third of the women were classified as nonresident clients.[1] This chapter considers the differences in helpseeking, first among racial groupings and then between shelter residents and nonresidents. The differences between the shelter residents and nonresidents also reflect our survivor hypothesis. Our discriminant analysis suggests that the high level of helpseeking remains constant among the racial groups, but some differences in services are warranted. The implications of these findings for shelter programming are also discussed.

Racial Differences among Shelter Women

Shelters for battered women face the racial questions that other human services have characteristically encountered (see Schechter 1982). Some of the basic questions in this regard are: Do shelter women of one race have more income and education than others, as one might assume? Does one group or another suffer more severe abuse and warrant specialized treatment for their injuries? Is there any group that is particularly reluctant to seek or obtain services? The research in the field of mental health suggests that the answer to all of these questions is yes. Racial minorities appear to be less inclined to contact formal help sources and less active in seeking help in general.

We further analyzed the Texas data to explore the differences among the white, black, and Hispanic shelter women in our sample. Selected background, abuse, and helpseeking variables were cross-tabulated by race and subsequently entered into a stepwise discriminant function to determine the most differentiating factors. In general, the white shelter women appear to be of higher socioeconomic status than the Hispanics but are comparable to the black women in this regard. However, the three racial groupings appear to have experienced similar severity of abuse and levels of helpseeking. These findings imply that programmatic and policy initiatives must address the lack of mobility espeically of the Hispanic women.

Research on Racial Differences

There has been very little empirical study of the racial differences among shelter residents, even though there has been much discussion of the matter among clinicians and activists (see, for example, White 1985). The extensive research on human service utilization by racial groups provides, however, some generalizations that may be applicable to shelter women (Block 1981; Fischer 1969; Cannon and Locke 1977; Kravits and Schneider 1975).

According to the mental health research, black women in shelters would tend to draw less on comprehensive service (Evans et al. 1986; Wood and Sherrets 1984) and rely more on friends and family for support (McKinlay 1975; McAdoo 1978; Neighbors 1984; Warren 1978). The research on Hispanics implies that Hispanic women in shelters tend to be the most disadvantaged economically and to be married longer and fewer times (Frisbie 1986). The Hispanic women are also more likely to tolerate more abuse, which would be reflected in less helpseeking. When they did seek help, they would characteristically be more likely to call on police.

A few studies on race and abuse suggest further that blacks and Hispanics are more likely to tolerate their abuse and receive more severe abuse than whites. The most notable of these studies is a race and class analysis of the National Family Violence Survey (N = 2, 143) conducted by Cazenave and Straus (1979). The authors conclude (p. 295): "The persistence of higher rates of spousal violence for the large income group containing the black working class, and for blacks in both occupational groups, suggests that even aside from income differentials black spousal violence is notably high."

A study of Mexican–American and white women in a Texas shelter (N = 50) found that both groups appeared to have experienced equivalent amounts of abuse. The Hispanic women, however, were more tolerant of the abuse and identified fewer types of behaviors as abusive (Torres in press). They were also more likely to recommend contacting the police than the white women.

The generalizations about racial influence, however, must be weighed with caution, according to other studies on intraracial differences. For instance, the current studies on black social networks demonstrate the complexity of racial differentiation influenced by a variety of family variables (Neighbors and Jackson 1984; Taylor 1986). Intraracial differences are apparent among Hispanics, as well. Marital stability is influenced by whether one is foreign- or native-born, the degree of acculturation, generation since immigration, religiosity, and available social supports (Keefe 1982). Moreover, it is argued that ethnicity is an emergent process influenced by one's social environment as well as by cultural attributes (Gelfand and Fandetti 1986).

Method

The racial analysis of the Texas data consists of bivariate cross-tabulations and discriminant analyses of the racial groupings. Cross-tabulations were computed for the background, abuse, and helpseeking variables with the different racial groupings (white, black and Hispanic). This served as a data reduction procedure and as a means for generating descriptive statistics of the groupings.[2] (See table 4–1 for representative cross-tabulations.)

Discriminant functions were then calculated to determine the combination of variables that most differentiate five possible racial combinations, or "partitions" of race groupings, that is, white versus black versus Hispanic; white versus black and Hispanic, and so on (see table 4–2). Thirty variables that were shown to be influential in the cross-tabulations (and were determined to be relatively independent from each other [r < .4]) were entered into a stepwise analysis. A subsequent discriminant analysis was conducted controlling for income. That is, a discriminant function was calculated for the white versus black versus Hispanic comparison in four combined income categories (Low = 0–$10,000; Medium = $10–20,000; High = $20–30,000; and Very High = $30,000 or more).

There are several qualifications that must be made of such an analysis of racial differences. One is that there is increasing differentiation within the racial groups themselves. The Hispanic women, in particular, are subject to different levels of acculturation (see Cuellar et al. 1980; Gelfand and Fandetti 1986). Second, the level of reporting bias is likely to differ among the groups and therefore distort the findings on abuse. As mentioned, Torres (in press) found that Hispanics reported a smaller range of abusive behaviors and were in general more tolerant of the abuse. Third, socioeconomic status also substantially confounds the racial differences, as our findings suggest, and raises problematic issues with regard to the relationship of race and class (see Petersen 1980).

Findings

Cross-Tabulations. The racial groupings appear to differ, as expected, in terms of the background variables for income and marital status (see table 4–1). The differences in terms of abuse, however, were minimal overall. Also, the helpseeking behaviors of the women, both before and during shelter, were relatively similar.[3]

In terms of combined income, 32 percent of the whites, 35 percent of blacks, and 52 percent of the Hispanics were below the poverty line. The black women tended, however, to have educational, occupation, and personal income levels comparable to the whites; these levels for both the whites and the blacks were substantially higher than for the Hispanics. The Hispanics characteristically were married the longest and had much lower education, employment, and job status. The white women, on the whole, were slightly older and had the fewest children.

Table 4–1
Cross-Tabulations of Variables by Race

	White	Black	Hispanic	Row Total
Total (column)	57%	15%	29%	100%
Background Variables				
Combined Income				
$10,000 or less	33	36	54	39
$10,001 to $20,000	35	39	32	35
$20,001 or more	32	25	15	26
$\chi^2 = 201.76$ (4); $p < .00001$				
Personal Income				
none	56	48	61	57
$5,000 or less	19	25	23	21
$5,001 to $10,000	14	15	12	13
$10,001 or more	10	12	4	9
$\chi^2 = 81.92$ (6); $p < .00001$				
Education				
Less than 12 years	41	29	63	45
High school diploma	39	44	26	36
Some post-high school/college	21	27	10	19
$\chi^2 = 339.39$ (4); $p < .00001$				
Times Married				
Never married	10	22	15	16
One time	52	64	66	61
Two times	28	11	14	17
Three or more	10	3	5	6
$\chi^2 = 55.13$ (6); $p < .00001$				
Length of Relationship				
Less than 1 year	17	15	10	15
1 to 5 years	49	49	41	46
More than 5 years	34	37	49	39
$\chi^2 = 115.19$ (4) $p < .00001$				
Number of Children				
0	14	11	7	11
1	27	24	21	25
2	31	30	27	30
3 or more	28	35	45	34
$\chi^2 = 154.76$ (6); $p < .00001$				
Abuse Variables				
Physical Abuse (most severe)				
Grabbed, pushed, slapped	17	11	15	16
Punched	15	17	14	15
Kicked	28	24	31	28
Weapons used	39	48	40	41
$\chi^2 = 44.71$ (6); $p < .00001$				
Duration of Abuse				
1 to 12 months	35	35	28	33
1 to 5 years	44	42	39	43
5 years or more	22	23	33	24
$\chi^2 = 78.67$ (4); $p < .00001$				

Table 4–1 continued

	White	Black	Hispanic	Row Total
Helpseeking Variables				
Previous Helpseeking				
0 to 2 sources	48%	44%	45%	47%
3 to 4 sources	33	36	35	35
5 to 10 sources	19	21	20	19
$\chi^2 = 7.39$ (4); Not sig.				
Care Sought (for injuries)				
none	21	18	22	21
1 source	59	16	25	16
2 sources	16	17	14	16
3 to 6 sources	21	23	14	19
$\chi^2 = 63.97$ (6); $p < .00001$				
Services to Be Continued				
none	36	34	37	35
1 to 2 services	40	35	35	38
3 to 8 services	25	31	29	27
$\chi^2 = 25.34$ (4); $p < .00001$				

The different racial groups of women reported receiving comparable kinds of physical, verbal, sexual, and child abuse. The outstanding exception was that black women more often (48 percent) reported having a weapon used against them, versus the white and Hispanic women (39 percent). The frequency of abuse was also relatively the same for all the groups (42 percent once a week). The Hispanic women, however, tended to report the longest duration of abuse (32 percent more than five years versus 21 percent for the whites and blacks).

In terms of helpseeking, the women from different racial groups sought about the same amount of different kinds of assistance prior to entering the shelter ("previous helpseeking"). Hispanic women, however, were the least likely to contact a friend, minister, or social service, suggesting their relative social isolation. A greater percentage of whites visited or phoned a social service, and more black women contacted a minister or police, as the mental health research suggests. An equal percentage of women previously contacted the shelter, left home, or obtained legal service.

The women obtained about the same number of different kinds of shelter services. (White women obtained on average a total of 3.0 of a possible 7 services, as opposed to 3.3 services for the Hispanic and black women.) Nevertheless, the white women had fewer children to service and more often had their own transportation. Sixty-two percent of the whites had their own cars, whereas only 40 percent of the nonwhite women did.

The whites, furthermore, expected to use fewer services after leaving the shelter, perhaps reflecting their greater resources. However, a smaller proportion of white women planned to live separate from their batterers despite their greater mobility (66 percent versus 71 percent and 73 percent). This may be a reflection of the proportion of white batterers in counseling.

Discriminant Analyses. The stepwise discriminant analysis of the variables verifies the combined influence of these variables in differentiating the racial grouping of battered women (table 4–2). Personal income, marital norms, and general violence remain relatively influential across different partitionings of the racial groups, except for the whites-versus-blacks partition. In this case,

Table 4–2
Discriminant Analyses of Partitioned Race Groups

	Partition[a]				
	W/B/H	W/BH	W/B	WB/H	W/H
Variable					
Combined income	.65	.55		.70	.70
Times married	.60	.65	.55	.40	.42
No personal income[b]	.41	.37		.42	.41
Relationship length	−.35	−.29		−.46	−.40
General violence	.31	.37	.37		.24
Abuse frequency	−.29	−.23		−.37	−.35
Previous abuse	−.21	−.27			−.19
Threatened killing[b]	.15			.21	.25
Previous helpseeking	.05		−.29	.18	
Batterer arrested[b]	.04	.18	.25		
Child abuse[b]	.04		−.22	.22	.17
Batterer in counseling[b]	.01		−.34		
Education	−.01		−.34		
Emergency room care[b]			−.26		
Weapons used[b]			−.19	.19	
Age of woman				.20	.21
Severe injury[b]			.29		
Function Statistics					
Eigenvalue	.22	.21	.21	.21	.26
Canonical Correlation	.43	.41	.42	.42	.45
Wilks' Lambda	.72	.83	.82	.83	.79
Chi square	88.96	52.12	39.49	52.07	53.10
Degrees of Freedom	26	8	12	11	10
Significance	.0001	.0001	.0001	.0001	.0001
Correct Classification	58%	62%	77%	73%	69%

Note: Thirty variables on background, abuse, and helpseeking were entered into a stepwise analysis for each partition. Fourteen variables were deleted as insignificant in all of stepwise analyses: woman's occupation, number of children, marital status, abused in previous relationship, severity of batterers' substance abuse, severity of physical abuse, severity of verbal abuse, threatened to harm children,[b] duration of the abuse, total kinds of care sought, total kinds of injuries, total number of shelter services obtained, planned living arrangements, and the batterer's response to the abuse.
[a]W = white; B = black; H = Hispanic.
[b]Dummy variables.

the income variables and length of relationship are not significant, while variables related to arrest, child abuse, and education are. Moreover, the discriminant results suggest that the most pronounced differences are between the whites and blacks, on the one hand, and the Hispanics, on the other, rather than between whites and nonwhites.

More specifically, the highest discriminant coefficients in the function for whites-versus-blacks-versus-Hispanics were for combined income (.65), times married (.60), no personal income (.41), length of the relationship (−.35), and general violence (.31). The weight of these variables shifts slightly in the whites-versus-blacks-and-Hispanics (or whites versus nonwhites) partition; the variable "times married" (.65) is the most influential instead of "combined income" (.55). Nevertheless, the influence of income (.70) is the greatest for the partitions of whites-and-blacks-versus-Hispanics and whites-versus-Hispanics.

The function statistics indicate that the power of the respective discriminant analyses is at best moderately strong. The whites-versus-Hispanics partition, however, is the strongest (eigenvalue = .26), accounting for .31 percent of the variance (Wilks' Lambda = .79). It is interesting that, despite a great range and number of variables used in the analysis, a substantial portion of the variance is still unexplained. Some of this may, no doubt, be accounted for by the cultural differences *within* racial groups and the general shortcomings of the abuse measures, mentioned in the discussion of qualifications.

The discriminant functions that control for income show comparable results both in terms of explanatory power and coefficient strength. Low, medium, and high income levels show "times married" to be equally as influential in differentiating the racial groups (.43, .64, .56), but "length of relationship" is not as influential (−.15, −.06, .12). The difference in "general violence" (−.35, −.52, .53, −.65) and "severity of injury" (−.27, .43, −.49, .38) among the racial groups, on the other hand, appears to increase when income level is controlled. Additional cross-tabulations, however, show that the most violent and most injured group varies from income level to income level. In sum, combined income or "class status" does not appear to appreciably alter the pattern of differences among the racial groups.

Implications

As might be expected, the racial groups differed most of all in terms of income-related variables. However, they differ very little in terms of abuse and help-seeking, as Bowker (1983) and Walker (1984) found in their studies of battered women. One interesting finding with regard to income is that the black shelter women were on a par with the whites in terms of personal income, and a greater proportion of them were employed. (Also, their batterers were less generally violent and had fewer previous arrests than with the whites.) One possible inference is that lower income blacks are not as likely to seek shelter and are underrepresented in this study. They may be more likely to rely on informal networks for support, as other research on human services utilization suggests.

A second, and probably more important, finding is the difference in marital norms, which appear to be related to socioeconomic status and duration of abuse. Specifically, Hispanic women appear to be bound by a norm of "loyal motherhood." They tend to be married younger, have larger families, and stay in relationships longer. They are similarly poorer, less educated, and longer abused than their counterparts.

These findings point particularly to the difficult position of the Hispanic women in shelters. These women appear to be burdened not only by language differences and discrimination but also by limited mobility due to larger families, less personal income, and more imposing marital norms. In sum, the white and black women appear to have more in common, suggesting that the significant differentiation does not necessarily fall along color lines.

The Hispanic women especially need more economic and educational supports to help them in their crisis, as well as in general. They need to be given priority in terms of housing, social welfare benefits, child care, and transportation. This need is compounded by the fact that a substantial portion of Hispanic women in Texas shelters are "undocumented citizens" and are not eligible for public assistance.[4] Much of the their aid must therefore come from church or private organizations devoted to assisting undocumented worker families.

In this light, shelters need to act as service centers for victims of economic disadvantage as well as abuse. This is apparent in the fact that nearly half of all the Texas shelter women have no personal income and at least a third come from families living below the poverty line. Other statewide studies have shown the disporportionate amount of abuse among lower income groups (Petersen 1980).

How shelters can more effectively respond to these economic needs remains problematic, especially given their limited resources and their crisis-oriented service. Shelters must expand to provide more extensive programs of economic assistance, as many have done, and other community agencies must give higher priority to aiding battered women. This ideal is unlikely, however, unless some substantial economic changes are made. Ultimately, social policies must be implemented that reduce the economic burdens of shelter women and women in general.

Shelter Residents and Nonresidents

While the helpseeking and abuse differences among racial groupings appear to be minimal, differences in this regard do exist between resident and nonresident shelter women. An increasing number of shelters have established services for battered women who do not reside in the shelter facility.[5] According to our Texas study, the nonresidents tend to come from a higher socioeconomic status, have been the victims of less frequent abuse, and have less generally violent batterers. As our survivor hypothesis suggests, they have also sought less help. In general, they appear to need less intensive service, less economic support, and more formally structured counseling and advisory services than the shelter residents.

Research on Inpatients and Outpatients

There has been little empirical investigation comparing shelter residents and nonresidents, in part because formalized nonresidential programs are still a relatively recent innovation. The research comparing "inpatients" and "outpatients" in other treatment settings is, however, well developed and offers some basis for speculation about shelter residents and nonresidents. The findings of the treatment studies, of course, have to be weighed with caution, since battered women may be more comparable to crime victims than mental health patients (Walker 1984).

The research literature shows that so-called outpatients tend to be more educated and have more social support (Kern et al. 1978; Penk et al. 1979; Skinner 1981). Alcoholic outpatients, for instance, score higher on intelligence and social adjustment tests but appear no more or less employed than inpatients (Skinner 1981).

The outpatient symptomatology also tends to be less severe. For instance, alcoholic outpatients, matched with comparable inpatients, reported less alcohol consumption and more severe symptoms (Skinner 1981). Outpatients also had fewer previous hospitalizations, but they did have more alcohol-related arrests (Kern et al. 1978).

One of the longstanding assertions in the treatment field is that outpatient services are at least as beneficial as inpatient services whenever safety and self-care are assured. A recent study of randomly assigned inpatients and outpatients with a range of mental disorders showed similar clinical outcomes (Dick et al. 1985). Also, outpatients were not found to be any more depressed after treatment than inpatients (Byerly and Carlson 1982).

Outpatients, moreover, incur one-third the cost and less degrading definitions of illness and continue more "normal" functioning in the community (Washburn et al. 1976). There may in fact be a bias in the community against former inpatients. For instance, school social workers were more likely to assign previous inpatients to more restrictive educational settings (Alexson and Sinclair 1986).

We might expect from these findings that shelter residents and nonresidents will be differentiated in terms of background and symptomatology and warrant different services. While there are safety issues that may preclude nonresident status for many battered women, the inpatient/outpatient research also suggests that there may be advantages to nonresident services and that such services should be expanded.

Method

We compared the Texas shelter residents and nonresidents in order to investigate these inpatient/outpatient differences. Our sample, in this instance, included shelter women from the six counties served by the state's five nonresident programs in existence between 1984 and 1985.[6] Shelter "residents" are defined as those clients who resided in the emergency shelter facility for at least three days. "Nonresidents" are those clients who received services from a formally instituted nonresident program operated by the shelter. They received services beyond crisis phone counseling, without residing in the facility.[7]

The analysis of the resident/nonresident differences was conducted similar to the one for racial differences. Cross-tabulations were used to identify influential variables and develop a descriptive overview of the sample (see table 4–3). A discriminant function was calculated in order to determine the most influential combination of differentiating variables.[8]

Gamma coefficients are also reported as a measure of the association between the cross-tabulated variables and to help identify the more influential variables (table 4–4). Furthermore, the cross-tabulated variables were controlled for the combined income of the battered woman and her batterer and for the frequency of the abuse.

In the discriminant analysis, twelve of the variables shown to be influential in the bivariate analysis were entered into the discriminant function using a stepwise method based on Wilks' Lambda (see table 4–5).[9] "No income" was included as a variable, because it appeared particularly influential as a control variable in the cross-tabulations.

Findings

Cross-tabulations. The cross-tabulations indicate that the nonresident women tend to be less economically dependent on their husbands (see table 4–3). They have higher income, education, and job status than the shelter residents. In fact, twice as many nonresidents (24 percent) as shelter residents (12 percent) made over $10,000 a year. At the other extreme, half of the nonresidents and nearly three-quarters (72 percent) of the residents were unemployed.

The differences in income were reflected in occupational and educational differences, as one might expect. For instance, the shelter residents were more likely to be homemakers (52 percent versus 33 percent), and more nonresidents reported being professionals or managers (17 percent versus 7 percent). Similarly, 40 pecent of the shelter residents and 28 percent of the nonresidents reported less than twelve years of education.

The nonresident women also had fewer and older children, which is likely to afford them more mobility. In fact, twice as many of the nonresidents did not have children (26 percent versus 13 percent). The age differences in the

Table 4–3
Cross-Tabulations for Income Amount and Source, Frequency of Abuse, and Planned Separate Living

	Shelter Resident	*Nonresident*
Income Amount of Client*		
None	56%	35%
$5,000 or less	20	17
$5,001–$10,000	13	24
$10,000+	12	24
Income Source of Client**		
Job/job training	28	51
Public assistance	7	10
Spouse/partner	18	12
None	47	26
Frequency of Abuse***		
Once	9	13
Once a month or less	25	34
2–3 times per month	19	25
Weekly/daily	47	28
Planned Separate Living****		
Return to batterer	19	20
Undetermined	12	36
Live separate from batterer	70	46

$*\chi^2 = 144.28$ (3) $p < .0001$.
$**\chi^2 = 131.93$ (3) $p < .0001$.
$***\chi^2 = 60.27$ (3) $p < .0001$.
$****\chi^2 = 125.45$ (3) $p < .0001$.

children appear to reflect the fact that nonresident women were generally older than the residents.

Both groups experienced similar kinds and severity of physical abuse and injury, but the residents were abused more frequently (47 percent versus 28 percent once a week to daily) and more often with weapons (51 percent versus 32 percent).[10] The nonresidents on average had endured abuse for a longer period of time (33 percent versus 23 percent for five years or more), perhaps because they were faced with less severe abuse. Moreover, nearly one-third (32 percent) of the residents had children who were abused, compared with less than one-fifth (18 percent) of the nonresidents.

The differences between the shelter and nonshelter women again bear out our survivor hypothesis. The shelter residents sought more different kinds of help, and probably more help in general (although no variable directly measured the amount of helpseeking). They reported, on average, five out of a total of eleven possible categories for "response to the abuse," as compared to an average of three reported by the nonresidents. It appears that the resident women took more assertive action in order to survive the more frequent abuse inflicted on them and their children.

The batterers of the residents and nonresidents did not significantly differ in their background. However, they are different in terms of the severity of their abuse, general violence, and criminality. The residents' batterers were nearly twice as likely to be destructive to belongings (45 percent versus 20 percent), abusive to animals (23 percent versus 15 percent), and violent toward non-family individuals (39 percent versus 21 percent). Moreover, half (51 percent) of the shelter residents' batterers had been arrested, as opposed to 38 percent of the nonresidents' batterers (38 percent and 26 percent had been convicted of some crime).

The more abusive tendencies of the residents' batterers are reflected further in their "response to the abuse." In eight of the "response to abuse" categories, from apologizing to threatening, residents' batterers exceeded the nonresidents by at least 10 percent. In fact, residents cited on average a total of five different categories of "response to abuse" as opposed to nonresidents' averages of three different categories. This suggests that the residents' batterers are more varied and inconsistent in their response to abuse.

Bivariate Association. The gamma coefficients suggest that the multilevel variables of income amount (.36) and source (.40), most severe verbal abuse (−.32), frequency of abuse (−.27), the batterer's response to the abuse (−.30), and planned living separately from the batterer (−.32) are the most strongly associated with shelter status (see table 4–4). The dichotomous variables for being employed (.43), abuse with weapons (−.32), child abuse (−.29), threats to harm child (−.29), and batterer violence outside the home (−.40) appear to be the most influential in differentiating the two groups.

Variables for the "client's race" and "violence witnessed" had no statistically significant influence on shelter status. The women were also not significantly differentiated by the kind of injury nor by the care they sought for the injury. Furthermore, the most severe general violence, alcohol abuse, and other background variables for the batterer (including income and education) had no significant relationship to the woman's shelter status.

Lastly, the role of "income amount" and "abuse frequency" are especially evident in their partial influence over the other background and abuse variables. When the cross-tabulations, summarized above, are controlled for income, the percentage differences for residents and nonresidents generally vanish or decrease in the low-income category (below $10,000 per year combined income). When the cross-tabulations are controlled for the frequency of abuse, the differences generally vanish for the "seldom" category (no more than once a year). This finding suggests that those women having a low income (46 percent of the sample) or those who were seldom abused (10 percent) were less likely to be differentiated by other variables.

Table 4–4
Gamma Coefficients for Cross-Tabulated Variables

Variable	Gamma	Chi Square (degrees of freedom)
Client Background		
Age of client	.22	27.86 (2)
Number of children	− .21	55.62 (3)
Age of youngest child	.20	10.44 (2)
Education of client	.18	26.26 (2)
Occupation of client	.30	89.78 (4)
Employed	.43*	93.89 (1)
Income amount of client	.36	144.28 (3)
Income source of client	.40	131.93 (3)
Length of relationship	.18	19.76 (2)
Abuse		
Physical abuse	− .17	52.72 (3)
Weapons used	− .32*	46.80 (1)
Verbal abuse	− .32	96.69 (3)
Threaten to harm child	− .40*	61.92 (1)
Frequency of abuse	− .27	60.27 (3)
Duration of abuse	.24	36.64 (2)
Child physical abuse	− .29*	20.84 (1)
Batterer's Behavior		
General violence	− .40	65.22 (3)
Arrested	− .24*	27.71 (1)
Response to abuse	− .30	149.86 (3)
Currently in counseling	− .32*	44.38 (2)
Client Helpseeking		
Previous helpseeking	− .15	26.35 (3)
Called shelter	− .48*	106.09 (1)
Shelter services obtained	− .15	26.35 (3)
Planned separate living	− .32	125.45 (2)

Not Significant
Combined income, Race of client, Times married, Abuse as child, Sexual abuse*, Injury, Care sought for injury, Batterer's substance abuse, and other background variables for batterer.

*Dichotomous variables.
$p < .0001$.

Discriminant Analysis. The stepwise discriminant analysis derived an optimal function of seven variables from a total of twelve (see table 4–5). As suggested in the bivariate analysis, the most influential variables, based on the standardized coefficients, are "general violence" (−.67), "no income" (−.51), and "duration of abuse" (.45). The women's "previous helpseeking," the presence of "child abuse," and the number of different issues related to the abuse also contribute to the resident/nonresident classification. As the reported statistics suggest, the final function is at least moderately powerful (eigenvalue = .28 and canonical R = .47) for this type of data. The cross-validated classification matrix showed a relatively high (74 percent) correct rate.

Table 4–5
Stepwise Discriminant Analysis for Shelter Residents
and Nonresidents

Predictor	Standardized Coefficient
General violence	– .67
No income for the client	– .51
Duration of abuse	.45
Child physical abuse	– .30
Issues related to abuse	.28
Frequency of abuse	.19
Age of client	.16

Function: Eigenvalue = .28; Canonical Corr. = .47; Wilks'
Lambda = .78; Chi sq. = 59.78 (d.f. = 8); Sig. = .0001

Classification: Resident 88%; nonresident 39%; overall 74%

Other Variables Entered: Client's education, Number of children,
Physical abuse, Threaten to harm child, Arrested

These discriminant results confirm that the nonresident women are most different in terms of having some income of their own, less frequent abuse, and less incidence of child abuse. The nonresidents have experienced abuse for a longer period, but, as mentioned, this may in part be related to their older age and less extensive abusiveness. The nonresident's batterers are less generally violent but have more issues related to their abuse, most of which are related to job pressures. Their abuse may, therefore, be more stress related (see Gondolf 1987b).

Implications

Summary. The shelter residents and nonresidents appear to be two distinct groups differentiated primarily by the victim's income, frequency of abuse, and batterer's general violence. The nonresidents, on average, have more education and fewer children, as well as higher incomes. Also, they and their children have experienced less severe abuse from less generally violent and arrested men. As our survivor hypothesis suggests, the nonresidents have in turn done less helpseeking. These differences are consistent with the differences observed between inpatient and outpatient groups in psychiatric and alcoholic treatment programs.

The striking differences between shelter residents and nonresidents have implications especially for shelter programs. Many of the shelter implications, however, might be extended to other formal help sources attempting to respond to the battered women. The socioeconomic differences, in particular, suggest that the two groups warrant not only different degrees of shelter but also different forms of counseling, referral, and advocacy services. The lower income status of the shelter residents clearly compounds their abuse problems. They are likely to face more barriers to employment and adequate housing. The nonresidents have more mobility due to their higher income and fewer children, which makes it easier for them to establish independent living.

The fact that the nonresidents experienced less frequent and less life-threatening abuse by no means minimizes the victimization of the nonresidents. It does, however, indicate that they are in less need of emergency shelter. Also, their less violent batterers appear to be less antisocial and more tractable, and therefore they may be more likely to be receptive to treatment. As it turns out, twice as many of the nonresidents' batterers as the residents' (20 percent versus 11 percent) were reportedly in counseling.

Programmatic Issues. Given the socioeconomic differences between shelter residents and nonresidents, shelters have several questions to weigh in programs development. For instance, do the shelters, or other social services for that matter, hire two differently trained staffs for the two different populations? The nonresident staff is more likely to face higher educated, working women. These nonresident women are likely to expect more formalized programming, such as appointments for meetings and more structured counseling, than is commonly offered in the more informal shelter setting. The nonresident staff is less likely to be called on for referral and advocacy, since its clients will have fewer economic and legal demands facing them. In fact, the nonresident services are likely to conform to the organizational structure of a more traditional social service agency.

These sort of staffing and organizational differences could present administrative challenges, especially for shelters founded on the egalitarian premises of the grass-roots–based battered women's movement (Schechter 1982). How is a balance between what amounts to two programs to be maintained? How should funding, status, and decisionmaking be disbursed over the two programs? Does the presence of two programs lead to competing philosophies as well? The answers to such questions obviously do not have to preclude shelter cohesiveness. But it appears that as shelters progress down the inevitable road toward specialized nonresident programs, such questions must be openly confronted.

Once a nonresident program is established, some other operational questions emerge. For instance, what factors should be considered in admitting women to one program or the other? The nonresidents in our sample were self-selected in that they did not specifically ask for shelter. However, nearly one-third of the nonresidents have experienced very severe abuse (in terms of kind and frequency) and would no doubt benefit from the shelter sanctuary.

On the other hand, to what degree should a nonresident program be used an an alternative to shelter? In our population, as many as 12 percent of those receiving nonresidential services were waiting for shelter or were former shelter residents. Can a nonresidential program adequately accommodate the overflow of shelter residents who are different in background, abuse, and need? Given that most shelters' residential programs are overflowing, it may make sense to devote resources to the more needy residents. While the nonresident programs are clearly more cost effective, the nonresidents are clearly in less life-threatening situations and have fewer children at risk.

In any case, there is clearly a large portion of more independent women who are not inclined to seek shelter but who are still in need of service and support. The efforts to reach these women will bring a more diverse group to shelters and expand, as well, the response to wife abuse. They will also raise increasingly difficult questions with regard to shelter priorities and operation.

Notes

1. Less than 4 percent of the sample was classified as of another race (that is, other than white, black, or Hispanic). This portion is not considered in this calculation or the analysis that follows, since it is too small for significant results. The nature of nonresident status may vary considerably among programs. Some programs, for instance, offer support to women on a follow-up basis or in lieu of unavailable sheltering. For the purposes of our analysis, only those women in one of the state's five formally established nonresident programs are considered. These programs comprise 29 percent of the clients at their respective shelters.

2. Those cross-tabulated variables with a significance level of $p < .00001$ were considered for the multivariate analysis and used to develop a description of the racial groupings of women. The designation of this high significance level attempts to compensate for inflation of chi square by the large sample size.

3. A summary of variables related to the batterers is as follows: The white batterers were more likely to use severe discipline and threaten to harm their children, and the wife abuse of the white batterers was also more often related to conflicts over the children, along with job pressures, financial problems, and unemployment. The Hispanic batterers abused alcohol the most (72 percent versus 68 percent for whites and 59 percent for blacks), and the black batterers tended to abuse drugs more often; whereas, the batterers of the white women were more generally violent and had been previously arrested and jailed more often than the blacks or Hispanics. Other research has shown Hispanic men to have greater alcohol abuse but not more antisocial behavior (Cahalan and Room 1974; Jessor et al. 1968), as our findings suggest. The batterers' response to the abuse (for example, apologize, deny, threaten, and so on) did not significantly differ.

4. There is no formal record of the total number of undocumented Hispanics in shelters. Shelter staff estimate that the proportion of Hispanic women who are undocumented may be as high as 40 percent.

5. The nonresident programs do a great deal to extend shelter services. For one, the nonresident services offer some consolation to many women who are denied shelter because the shelter is at capacity. Urban shelters may turn away as many as 85 percent

of their callers because they are filled to capacity (Schechter 1982). Second, the nonresident services appear to assist a new group of women who formerly were not inclined to seek shelter residence. These women may have managed to obtain safety through some other means or have been unwilling or unable to leave their current residences.

6. The number of battered women (physically abused and over eighteen years old) in the final sample is 1,482 residents (71 percent) and 650 nonresidents (29 percent), for a total of 2,132.

7. Both categories are self-determined rather than assigned by the staff. That is, the women referred themselves to resident or nonresident status. Two small subgroups of women that did not fit this criteria were deleted from the sample: (1) women who indicated that they were seeking shelter (5 percent) but who were assigned to nonresident status because of insufficient shelter space, and (2) women who were transferred from shelter to nonresident status in order to make room for someone else (7 percent). The statistics on this deleted group of women are comparable to the shelter residents rather than the nonresidents. (Only 3 percent of the nonresidents in the final sample, and 13 percent of the residents, had previously visited the shelter.)

8. The severity of abuse variables (collapsed into four-levels) and dichotomous categorical variables were cross-tabulated with resident/nonresident status (see table 4–3). Given the number of comparisons and effect of the large sample size on the p-value, a conservative p-value ($p < .0001$) was chosen to compensate for inflation of the experimentwise alpha level.

9. The variables shown to be influential in table 4–4 were excluded from the discriminant analysis if they violated the assumptions of discriminant analysis. That is, the "influential" variables were not included if their distributions were skewed when converted into a full ordinal scale or interval index, or if they were highly correlated with other independent variables. "No income" was chosen as the best indicator for the income-related variables because of its strong influence as a control variable in the cross-tabulations. The helpseeking variables were deleted because they were shown to be dependent on background and abuse variables (Gondolf et al. in press). The initial discriminant function was computed with a random subsample of 500 and cross-validated with another subsample of equal size.

10. These differences in abuse and socioeconomic status are even greater for clients in the longest operating and most advanced nonresident program. This particular shelter had one-third of its 340 clients as nonresidents. In nearly all of the ten categories of physical abuse, there were 20 percent more of the shelter residents who reported having experienced that particular kind of abuse. For instance, only 17 percent of the nonresidents, as opposed to 45 percent of the residents, reported having been abused with weapons. In terms of injury, twice as many shelter residents (54 percent) reported receiving head injuries. This shelter's nonresidents appeared to be of even higher socioeconomic status than the nonresidents statewide, suggesting that its nonresident program was attracting those who may previously have avoided the perceived stigma of shelter contact. These findings for the advanced nonresident program seem to indicate that the residents and nonresidents will appear less alike as programs mature.

5
Intervention with Batterers

In this chapter we examine the batterers and the principal intervention used to stop them—police action. The first section develops a typology of four different types of batterers, using a cluster analysis. The typology indicates that a substantial portion of the batterers are severely antisocial, besides being severely abusive, and are unlikely to be unresponsive to jailing and batterer counseling. As our hypothesis suggests, women tend to seek more help in response to these men. The question remains, however: What interventions are appropriate or effective for the various types of batterers?

The second section examines police action as one of the primary help sources solicited by women in response to severe abuse. Our discriminant functions suggest that police are responding more to the antisocial behavior of the batterer than to the wife abuse. The implications for improving police as a help source are raised at the conclusion of the chapter.

A Typology of Batterers

Men who batter women have frequently been cast in "monolithic" terms. In many of the accounts from shelter women, batterers appear as sadistic psychopaths with little or no humanity (Walker 1979). In the clinical reports of men in batterer programs, batterers are often presented as "victims" of parental abuse or neglect and responsive to counseling (Gondolf 1984).

Our findings suggest that there may be different types of batterers in terms of the severity of their abuse and antisocial behavior. At one extreme is a substantial portion of generally violent and severely abusive men who are unlikely to be responsive to short-term counseling. At the other extreme, a portion of the men appear to be less severe in their abuse and likely to respond to it with profuse apologies, as the "cycle of violence" notion suggests (Walker 1979).

In sum, many of the battered women face men who are highly antisocial besides being severely abusive. While batterers may share some underlying characteristics, some may warrant more comprehensive intervention and more precautions to assure the safety of the battered women.

Research on Batterers

In the last five years, a series of empirical studies on men who batter have endeavored to refine our clinically based profiles of batterers. This research has been made possible, in large part, by the development of batterer programs and increased police action in domestic violence cases. As a result of these interventions, a formerly elusive population has been identified and is now more accessible to researchers.

Most of the research on the batterer has been directed toward establishing the commonalities among batterers (for example, see Bernard and Bernard 1984; Goldstein and Rosenbaum 1985; Neidig et al. 1986; Rosenbaum and O'Leary 1981). This research remains, however, largely inconclusive and somewhat contradictory, according to at least two reviews of the literature (Edleson et al. 1985; Hotaling and Sugarman 1986).[1]

The difficulty in deriving a conclusive batterer profile may be, in part, a reflection of the differences among batterers. The fledgling effort to differentiate batterers offers some preliminary typologies based either on the batterer's personality or on his behavior. The typologies based on the batterer's personality include both clinical and empirical assessments. Drawing on clinical observations of batterer's emotional needs, Elbow (1977) characterized the controller, defender, approval seeker, and incorporator types of batterer.

Hamberger and Hastings (1986) more recently formulated an empirically based typology of batterers using the MCMI on 204 program participants. Their factor analysis indicated three major personality categories: narcissistic/antisocial personality disorder, schizoidal/borderline personality disorder, and passive dependent/compulsive personality disorder. An "Anger Inventory" showed differences in the batterers' proneness to and expression of anger, as well. These findings led the authors to conclude that there is "no unitary batterer profile."

The typologies based on batterers' behavior are less refined. Both Walker (1984) and Fagan et al. (1983), in analyzing data from battered women, found evidence of generally violent batterers. Shields and Hanneke (1983) introduced a typology of men's violence in their exploratory study based on interviews with 85 husbands identified by social services as "violent men" (as opposed to only batterers). They identified three patterns of violence in their sample: "family-only" violent men, "nonfamily" violent men, and "generally violent" husbands.

Snyder and Fruchtman (1981) developed an empirically based typology of wife abuse based on a cluster analysis of intake data from 119 shelter women. While this study specifically describes different "types" of battered women, it does suggest a differentiation of batterer violence as well. It noted three groupings of women: victims of sporadic violence with a fairly stable relationship, victims of severe unrelenting violence, and victims of extensive child abuse with infrequent wife abuse.

In sum, the research on batterers presents at best a vague profile along with indications that batterers may be differentiated by personality or behavior. Most of this research is based on information derived from batterers in treatment programs. Following these leadings, we developed a typology of the batterers of the shelter women. Our typology was derived using the batterer's abusive and antisocial behavior reported by the women. As discussed in chapter 1, this reporting is likely to be more reliable than that of the batterers. Also, a behavior typology as opposed to a typology based on personality types may be more relevant to the safety and helpseeking of the women.

Cluster Analysis

To develop our typology, we used a cluster analysis method which sorts the cases into statistically distinct groups.[2] Cross-tabulations were then used to determine the outstanding features of each cluster. Finally, the cross-tabulation of the clusters was presented to three clinicians, who were asked to pose a descriptive typology based on the data.

More specifically, the cluster analysis was conducted using the twelve variables of batterer abuse and antisocial behavior. The abuse variables included the weighted scores for physical abuse, verbal abuse, the batterer's response to the abuse, the injury inflicted, and child abuse. The antisocial variables were the weighted scores for substance abuse, general violence, and arrest record. Five ordinal variables related to abuse were also used in the subsequent analysis: frequency of abuse, duration of abuse, frequency of child abuse, duration of child abuse, and severity of sexual abuse. The solution with four distinct clusters was determined to be the optimal one.[3] (See table 5–1 for a partial listing and distribution of these variables.)

Cross-tabulations of categorical and dichotomous variables were computed for the four clusters, in order to develop descriptive data useful in interpreting the cluster solution.[4] The tabulated variables included descriptive abuse and antisocial variables (table 5–2), batterer's background variables (table 5–3), and variables related to the victim's response to the abuse (table 5–4).

Lastly, a typology was developed through clinician's interpretations of the descriptive data. The data for the clusters were presented to three clinicians—one from a psychiatric hospital, another from an alcohol and drug program, and the last one from a domestic violence program. The clinicians were asked to characterize and label the clusters; a consensus of their appraisals was derived by questioning the clinicians about contradictary interpretations until a consensus was reached. This procedure was introduced as a means of compensating for the varying interpretations that cluster solutions sometimes present and to assure a clinical grounding for the typology.[5]

Table 5–1
Cross-Tabulation of Batterer Abuse and Antisocial Scores

	Cluster				
	I	*II*	*III*	*IV*	*Total*
Cluster % of sample	5%	32%	30%	33%	100%
Physical Abuse*					
low	23	0	25	60	28
medium	59	22	67	38	42
high	18	78	9	3	30
Verbal Abuse*					
low	14	6	20	39	21
medium	46	45	60	54	53
high	40	49	20	7	27
Injury*					
low	0	2	23	41	21
medium	5	36	67	53	49
high	95	62	10	6	29
Response to Abuse (severity)*					
low	0	7	0	53	20
medium	5	58	50	46	50
high	96	34	50	0	30
Substance Abuse*					
low	22	46	50	58	51
medium	33	42	43	34	39
high	44	13	7	8	10
General Violence*					
low	5	12	25	42	24
medium	40	60	50	47	53
high	55	28	25	10	24
Previous Arrests*					
low	18	34	41	49	41
medium	14	31	35	31	32
high	68	35	24	35	27

Note: These cross-tabulations represent a portion of the twelve abuse and antisocial variables used to calculate the clusters. The distributions of the additional cross-tabulations reflect those above.
*$p < .0001$.

Cluster Findings

The cluster analysis established four distinct clusters that ranged from severely abusive and extremely antisocial men, at one extreme, and less abusive and more apologetic batterers, at the other extreme. In various cluster solutions, the two clusters with the most severe abuse and antisocial behavior were the most stable. The most severely abusive cluster comprised between 4 and 7 percent of the cases in the solutions of three to seven clusters. The next most severe cluster represented from 27 to 35 percent of the cases in the various cluster solutions. In the solution of four clusters, the clusters respectively comprised 5, 32, 30, and 33 percent of the sample.

The cross-tabulations of the four clusters reveal little difference in terms of background variables (see table 5–3). At most, the four clusters may be statistically different in terms of education, and Cluster I and Cluster II may be differentiated from the other clusters by race, income, and family size, but not substantially. The most distinguishing variables are the injury and arrest scores used in calculating the clusters (see table 5–1). Ninety-six percent of Cluster I was comprised of cases that scored "high" in injury, while only 6 percent of Cluster IV scored high. Sixty-eight percent of Cluster I was in the high category of arrests, and only 17 percent of Cluster IV. Similarly, Clusters I and II were characterized by higher levels of other abuse and violent behaviors in the cross-tabulations (see table 5–2). For instance, 95 percent of Cluster I generally responded to the abusive incident by threatening to "do it again," as

Table 5–2
Cross-Tabulation of Batterer Descriptive Variables

	Cluster				
	I	*II*	*III*	*IV*	*Total*
Cluster % of sample	5%	32%	30%	33%	100%
Length of Relationship (more than five years)**	36	38	45	28	37
Weekly Abuse*	68	50	49	35	46
Kicked*	46	96	56	32	61
Weapon Used*	36	80	26	17	43
Sexual Abuse*	59	36	34	20	31
Child Abuse**	46	26	24	17	23
Threaten or Blame (in response to abuse)*	91	62	76	9	50
Broken Bones*	46	23	7	5	13
Drug Abuse*	60	37	28	22	30
Nonfamily Violence*	68	54	43	25	42
Arrest for Nonfamily Violence*	64	23	15	13	19

n = 550.

Note: These variables represent a portion of the dichotomous variables cross-tabulated for descriptive purposes. Cross-tabulations were also calculated for different kinds of physical abuse, injury, care for the injury, discipline of children, response to abuse, issues related to abuse, and other arrests and violence.

*$p < .0001$.

**$p < .01$

***N.S.

Table 5–3
Cross-Tabulation of Batterer Background Variables

	Cluster				
	I	*II*	*III*	*IV*	*Total*
Cluster % of sample	5%	32%	30%	33%	100%
Race**					
White	50	47	57	54	52
Black	14	22	15	17	18
Hispanic	27	28	25	24	26
Education*					
Less than 12 years	38	51	33	43	43
High school diploma	38	29	49	42	40
College	24	19	17	15	18
Income**					
$5,000 or less	15	28	20	28	25
$5,001–10,000	55	47	46	43	46
$10,001 or more	30	25	34	29	30
Children**					
None	10	13	11	8	11
1 child	43	23	28	29	27
2 children	29	33	26	26	29
3 children	19	14	20	23	19
4 or more	0	18	15	14	15

n = 550.
Note: Cross-tabulations for batterer's age, occupation, times married, and length of relationship were also insignificant.
*$p < .01$.
**N.S.

opposed to only 9 percent of Cluster IV. Despite these behavioral extremes, the percentage (14 percent) of batterers in counseling comprising Cluster I and II is comparable to Cluster III and IV.

Cross-tabulations with variables related to the victim's response to the abuse confirm the findings about helpseeking discussed in the previous chapters: The women with the most severely abusive batterers are the most active helpseekers (see table 5–4). Seventy-three percent of the victims in the most abusive cluster (Cluster I) had sought seven to thirteen different help sources, as opposed to only 9 percent of those in the least abusive Cluster IV. There is, however, surprisingly little difference in the victim's living arrangements upon leaving the shelter.

Typology

The following typology is an attempt to characterize the cluster findings described above. The batterer "types," patterning the clusters, range from the most

Table 5–4
Cross-Tabulation of Women's Response Variables

	Cluster				
	I	II	III	IV	Total
Cluster % of sample	5%	32%	30%	33%	100%
Called Police*	64	60	56	42	53
Took Legal Action*	46	24	26	8	20
Help Sources Contacted* 6–13 sources	73	34	28	9	26
Living Arrangements** Return to batterer	18	19	18	25	21
Undetermined	5	12	10	4	9
Live with friend	50	45	40	53	46
Live on own	27	24	31	19	25

*$p < .0001$.
**$p < .05$.

to the least severe abuse and antisocial behavior. The terms used to identify the batterer types attempt to reflect the clinical assessment commonly associated with the behaviors characterizing each cluster.

Type I—The Sociopathic Batterer. This type of batterer is extremely abusive of his wife and children and has inflicted the most severe injury. He is most likely to have been abusive sexually as well. Moreover, this batterer's violence extends beyond the home. In fact, he might be characterized as sociopathic, considering his previous arrests, extrafamily violence, animal abuse, and severe substance abuse. This batterer's victim has actively sought help, including calling the police and obtaining legal assistance.

Type II—The Antisocial Batterer. This type of batterer is also extremely abusive physically. However, his abuse has been less injurious than the sociopathic batterer's, even though he is most likely to have abused with weapons. While he is likely to have been violent outside the family, his arrest record is lower than that of the sociopathic batterer. Interestingly, he is just as likely to be in counseling as the less severe batterers.

Type III—The Chronic Batterer. This type of batterer has committed severe verbal and physical abuse that has been less injurious than that of the sociopathic and antisocial batterer. He is particularly less likely to have used weapons than the other severe batterers. His verbal abuse, marital rape, and child abuse, as well as his extrafamily violence, are also less severe than those of the antisocial batterer. This batterer, nevertheless, tends to threaten or blame his victim following the abuse.

Type IV—The Sporadic Batterer. This type of batterer's physical abuse is minimal compared to the others, and his verbal abuse and sexual abuse are the least severe. His physical abuse occurs with less frequency than the others, and he might be characterized as being apologetic after abusive incidents. Moreover, he is the least likely to have alcohol problems and has had little contact with the police. His victim has sought the least amount of help and is most likely to return.

Implications

The typology of batterers suggests that a substantial portion of batterers— over a third of shelter women's batterers—might be considered "sociopathic" or "antisocial," as well as severe abusers. The identification of sociopathic and antisocial batterer types substantiates earlier studies based on victims' reports which point to the presence of a "violent prone" personality (Walker 1984) and an association between severity of abuse and general violence (Fagan et al. 1983). It also confirms the preliminary attempts to construct a behavioral typology of batterers (Shields and Hanneke 1983) and the more recent research on personality types that include a sociopathic/narcissistic type of batterer, whose abuse is not anger driven (Hamberger and Hastings 1986).[6]

While it is important not to stereotype batterers as unusually "deviant" men, we should also not overlook the fact that many batterers are possibly sociopathic or antisocial personalities, as our typology suggests. It is unlikely that counseling programs or jailing are going to affect the sociopathic and antisocial type batterers. In fact, these men are "system failures" in that they have been largely untouched by the system despite a history of socially undesirable and criminal behavior.

In sum, many battered women face another formidable obstacle, besides severe abuse and poverty. They face batterers who are generally violent, substance abusers, and have criminal records. Several considerations are therefore needed in intervening with the batterer.

First, batterer and battered women programs need to take the differences in batterers into account. Batterer programs may actually do better to reject the antisocial or sociopathic type batterers from counseling in order to avoid presenting another false hope to women. The hard fact may be that many of these batterers are beyond the scope of conventional treatment, especially those treatments that focus largely on anger control.

Conversely, more has to be done through shelters to assure the separation of especially the sociopathic and antisocial batterers from their victims. There is some evidence to suggest that victims of the sociopathic and antisocial batterers are just as likely to return to these extremely dangerous batterers as victims of the other types of batterers. This may in part be because these men are just as likely to have attended counseling as the other types of batterers, largely as a result of court mandate, and the fact, discussed in the following chapter, that enrollment in counseling is the most influential factor in a woman's return to the batterer.

Second, our social services need to address especially the multiproblem batterers in a more systematic fashion. The sociopathic and antisocial batterers, in particular, need a variety of interventions, including substance abuse and mental health treatment as well as severe restraint for their criminality. It is unlikely that especially the sociopathic batterers will change unless they are subjected to comprehensive residential care, much like the detoxification programs used for many alcoholics.

Also, the social services and law enforcement agencies dealing with antisocial behavior must be charged to intervene more decisively with antisocial men. Evidently these help sources are facing a substantial portion of abusers that they do not identify. They also appear to be treating a number of antisocial men without affecting their abusive behavior.

The fact that so many abusers have previously been antisocial without being deterred should in itself discourage battered women from seeking help. Why should they expect intervention for their batterer's abuse when there has been little effective intervention for the batterer's antisocial behavior in general? Our findings, however, suggest the opposite. Despite the system failure represented by the antisocial nature of so many batterers, battered women seek more help rather than less in the face of more antisocial batterers.

Police Action with Batterers

Given the proportion of antisocial batterers, it would certainly make sense that many women contact the police for help. Many of the batterers, as suggested above, are well beyond the influence of personal persuasion or informal help sources. According to our study, however, police action appears only secondarily to address the abuse. The batterer's antisocial conduct (for example, other arrests, alcohol abuse, and general violence) appears to be the most influential factor in the police action. Yet, in at least 20 percent of the cases, the batterers were not particularly antisocial but still committed severe abuse.

Research on Police and Wife Abuse

Police action in wife abuse cases has received tremendous attention in recent years. The attention is related in part to the publicized findings that arrest is an effective deterrent (Sherman and Berk 1984). Yet only about 10 percent of domestic violence cases result in arrests, even though there are grounds for arrest in well over half of these cases (Bowker 1982). As many as 61 percent of the requests for arrest were refused, according to Pagelow's (1981) study of four hundred shelter women. Even in states with mandatory arrest laws, there is as little as 40 percent compliance (Ferraro 1985).

This poor implementation may be related to the tendency of police to "handle" cases, as Worden and Pollitz (1984) conclude. A number of researchers (for instance, Bittner 1974; Black 1980; and Webster 1973) have argued that police engage in a complex process of "handling" cases, often irrespective of legal circumstances. That is, they tend to contain or manage the immediate situation facing them upon arrival, instead of responding to the crime that brought them there. In the process, the police exercise a good deal of discretion in implementing the law.

Much has been made of the predisposition of police that influences their handling of abuse cases. The officers' individual attitudes and own family situation have been shown to influence police response to wife abuse, according to a number of studies using validated instruments (see Stith 1987). Dobash and Dobash (1979), examining Scottish arrests, asserted that police were particularly unlikely to make arrests in domestic violence cases because of their sexist attitudes.

How these predispositions are enacted is suggested in the study of the situational factors associated with police action. Worden and Pollitz (1984) constructed a regression function of dummy variables indicating that the following variables contribute to the batterer being arrested: a formal arrest request, the male's drinking, violence alleged by the female only, and the incident being reported by other than the victim. The severity of injury and race of the victim showed little or no effect. Additionally, their findings were relatively consistent across different orientations of police officers ("crime fighters" versus "problem solvers") and were replicated with observational data by Berk and Loseke's (1980) arrest study based on police records (N = 262 of 730 domestic violence cases).

Berk and Newton (1986), in their replication of the Minneapolis Police Study (Sherman and Berk 1984), developed a logistic regression for "propensity for arrest" that showed a batterer's belligerence, past convictions, the particular police department, and the batterer's drinking to be factors in arrest. The proportion of arrests does not appear to be influenced by the marital status of the victim (Erez 1986).

In sum, arrests in wife abuse cases appear to turn on extralegal factors. More needs to be done, however, to identify the situational factors specifically involved in police action, especially those related to the batterer's behavior. The research on police intervention needs to consider forms of police action other than arrest, such as mediation, referral, and doing nothing. It might also benefit from using battered women's reporting, as our study does, instead of police records and observations, which are known to be severely distorted (Adrian and Mitchell 1978).

Method

To examine the role of police intervention in the helpseeking process, we analyzed the different police actions for those women who contacted the police,
using a series of discriminant analyses. More than half (53 percent) of the Texas
shelter women had previously called the police for help, as opposed to one-
third of the Bowker (1982) sample of formerly battered women. The callers
were distinguished from the noncallers by a higher level of helpseeking and
more generally violent and previously arrested batterers, but not by race or
income. We attempted to examine what factors contributed to the kind of help
or "police action" they received from contacting the police.

Police action was represented with five major categories of possible interventions ranging from the least to most severe: "did nothing," "mediated," "provided transportation," "forced batterer to leave," and "arrested batterer." The
variable was constructed from a multiple-response question: "The last time
the police arrived during or after an abusive incident, what actions did they
take?" The most "severe" category reported by the interviewee was recorded
as the "police action."[7]

As described in chapter 3, discriminant analyses were conducted to identify the most influential combination of background and abuse variables in
differentiating the police actions. Twenty-five variables, ten of which were
dummy variables, were entered in a stepwise procedure for four sets of police
action categories (see table 5–6).[8]

First, the "arrested" versus "not arrested" comparison was drawn, similar
to the Berk and Loseke (1980) study. Second, a discriminant function was computed for the three principal police actions comparable to those studied in the
Minneapolis Police Study (Sherman and Berk 1984): mediation, forcing the
batterer to leave, and arresting the batterer.

Third, the "did nothing" category was added to these three. Fourth, the
four major categories for "most severe" police action were computed. That is,
"provided transportation" was added to the previous set of categories, and the
"did nothing" category was deleted. This latter partitioning was employed in
order to account for the nonlinear effect of the "did nothing" category when
added sequentially to all of the other categories.

Discriminant Findings

The battered women mentioned an average of three different police actions
out of nine possible categories on the multiresponse question for police action
(see table 5–5). Nearly a third of the women received mediation or referral,
and nearly half were advised of legal rights. However, relatively few of the batterers were arrested, despite the glaring severity of the cases. The 15 percent

Table 5–5
Multiple Responses for Police Actions

Did nothing	32%
Mediated	30
Referred	30
Provided transportation	28
Advised rights	46
Warned batterer	24
Froced batterer to leave	9
Arrested batterer	15

$\bar{x}$ = 2.7 categories mentioned

Note: This table includes the multiple responses for the categories prior to constructing the "most severe" police action used in the discriminant analyses.

arrest rate for the Texas sample was actually higher than the range of arrest rates noted in previous studies (6–13 percent).

The stepwise discriminant functions suggest overall that batterers who have other arrests, abuse alcohol prior to their wife abuse, are extremely verbally abusive, and inflict severe injuries will receive more severe police action (see table 5–6). That is, the variables most related to the batterer's antisocial behavior are the most consistently influential in the analyses. The "previously arrested" variable is, for instance, the most influential variable in three out of the four functions for different sets of police actions, as its discriminant coefficients indicate (.63, .63, .57). In the "nonarrest versus arrest" function, alcohol abuse (.51), verbal abuse (.52), and nonfamily violence (.45), along with injuries (.49), are primarily responsible for the differentiation. The other abuse-related variables were conspicuously deleted from the stepwise analysis or marginally influential, as is the case with most of the background variables.

The influence of the antisocial variables is further indicated in their cross-tabulation with the five major police actions. As suggested in the discriminant function, the "did nothing" cases were less likely than "arrested" cases to abuse alcohol when battering (65 percent versus 84 percent), to be violent against others (36 percent versus 53 percent), and to have other arrests (55 percent versus 89 percent) (see table 5–7).

However, the "did nothing" cases, which accounted for 20 percent of the "most severe" police actions, were more comparable on several factors to the "arrested" and "forced" categories than the "mediated." Most important, the "did nothing" cases were more likely to have a weapon used on them (53 percent versus 39, 48, and 50 percent) and to have received threats against their lives (see table 5–7). Their injury and duration of abuse was also similar to the arrested cases.

In sum, the women in the "police did nothing" category were severely enough abused to expect more severe police action, but their batterers were less

Table 5–6
Discriminant Analysis for Factors of Police Actions

	Police Actions			
Factor	NA/A	M/F/A	N/M/F/A	M/T/F/A
Other arrests*	.31	.63	.63	.57
Alcohol abuse*	.51	.37	.28	.36
Verbal abuse	.52	.02		.13
Injuries	.49	.25		.15
Nonfamily violence arrest*	.45			
Threats about child*		.25	.39	.11
Helpseeking		.24	.09	.39
Number of children		.20	.08	.23
Previously called police*		.19	.08	.04
General violence		.11	.04	.07
Emergency room care*		.11	.02	.14
Physical abuse		.18		.28
Duration of abuse	.28			
Batterer unemployed*	.24			
Woman's age		.01		
Police arrival time			.49	
Racial minority			.19	
Weapons used*			.15	
Personal income*			.13	
Married*			.13	
Eigenvalue	.16	.14	.25	.15
Canonical corr.	.27	.35	.45	.36
Wilks' Lambda	.86	.80	.71	.80
Chi square	24.83 (8)	124.68 (24)	236.64 (39)	153.99 (36)
Significance	.001	.00001	.00001	.00001
Correctly classified	84%	62%	51%	50%

NA = not arrested; A = arrested; M = mediated; F = forced batterer to leave; N = did nothing; T = provided transportation.

generally violent, less criminal, and less alcohol abusing men than those in the other categories. The negative impact of "did nothing" on the women is indicated in the high dissatisfaction expressed by the women in these cases (only 14 percent were positive about the police action).

There are at least two plausible explanations for the apparent oversight on the part of the police. One, the did-nothing cases were comprised of a higher percentage of upper-income women (19 percent made more than $10,000). Police may feel that these higher income women could take care of themselves. Two, the variable for police response time indicates that police tended to have a slower response rate in the did-nothing cases. The police may have arrived too late in these cases; the batterer may have sufficiently calmed down or left by then.

Table 5–7
Cross-Tabulations of Police Actions by Categorical Variables[a]

	Police Actions					
	Nothing	Mediate	Transpo.	Forced	Arrest	Average
Background						
$10,000 income or more	19%	12%	13%	9%	10%	12%****
Abuse Related						
Weapons used	54	39	44	48	50	49****
Head injuries	60	46	65	57	62	58***
Emergency room	36	25	34	45	43	39**
Child abuse	29	23	21	28	30	28****
Batterer Behavior						
Alcohol abuse	63	66	69	77	84	75*
Nonfamily viol.	36	38	38	51	53	46**
Other arrests	55	68	62	63	89	73*
Threaten harm	38	42	46	43	58	48*
Other						
Legal help	27	22	24	36	38	33**
Police arrival (30 + minutes)	26	11	12	10	9	14*
Positive assessment of police	14	38	57	58	66	49*
Percentage of Sample	20	13	18	16	34	

Nothing = did nothing; Mediate = mediated couple; Transpo. = transportation provided to client; Forced = forced batterer to leave; Arrest = arrested batterer; Average = variable average.
[a]These categorical variables are those that registered statistically significant differences among the police actions.

    *$p < .00001$.
    **$p < .005$.
    ***$p < .01$.
    ****$p < .05$.

Implications

The police seem to be responding more to the antisocial nature of the batterers and less to the act of wife abuse itself. The belligerent and hostile batterers are more likely to be arrested, which is encouraging given that these men also tend to be the most severe abusers. However, the police in these cases may be attempting to manage the batterers' unruliness and protect themselves, rather than considering the potential lethality of these antisocial men as abusers. In other words, the police may be reacting more to the immediate dangerousness of these men than to the abuse they inflicted on women.

This scenario is compatible with the notion that the police use arrests, and other police actions, to "handle" the world of complex, extralegal circumstances—particularly the disruptive antisocial behavior at the site of a crime. It also supports the study of police arrest in domestic violence cases (Berk and Loseke 1980), which suggests that the more arrest-prone men are the most likely to be arrested.

This handling of the batterer's antisocial behavior serves police well, with one exception. There are a substantial number of cases in which less antisocial batterers have committed abuse as severe as the "arrested" cases. Moreover, the level of abuse throughout the sample was sufficiently extreme to warrant severe police action on the basis of legal definitions alone.

Therefore, the handling of antisocial men must be extended to the apprehension of wife abusers, especially those sporadic and chronic abusers who are less antisocial yet still very abusive. Decisive intervention is required to interrupt what will otherwise recur and escalate. To accomplish this, more is required than sensitizing the police to the issues of wife abuse. A procedural reorientation is also needed to help police move beyond their tendency to handle the immediate situation.

In sum, the police may be a logical and necessary help source to contact in the event of abuse. However, police intervention is limited in the assistance it can offer, given the types of batterers that police encounter. Severe police action is likely to be the most effective with the sporadic and chronic batterers who have little previous contact with the police. Also the less severe violence of the sporadic batterers is more easily interrupted by police before it escalates to the level of the chronic or antisocial batterers.

The police, however, tend to take more severe action with the antisocial batterers. Yet these men, as mentioned above, are less likely to be responsive to the intervention. The police action, very simply, is not as likely to have a deterrent effect, given these men's previous police contacts and apparent unresponsiveness to singular interventions. Consequently, many women are left with no alternative but to escape the man through their own efforts. Their best source of help at this point is a women's shelter.

Notes

1. The research has consistently identified lower self-esteem and lower masculinity scores among batterers, but this has conflicted with the clinical observations of "machoism" in batterers (Walker 1979). The self-report of "reformed" batterers suggests a "failed macho complex" that may explain this apparent inconsistency (Gondolf and Hanneken 1987). These batterers appear to overcompensate for what they perceive to be their failure to live up to the masculine sex role stereotype.

2. A K-means clustering algorithm (SPSSX Quick Cluster) was employed, since it is designed to accommodate a large number of cases and variables. K-means clustering produces a designated number of clusters through an agglomeration method that assigns cases to the nearest cluster centers and updates the center for each new case. An agglomerative hierarchical procedure (based on squared Euclidean distances and an unweighted average linkage) was, also, conducted for the purposes of validation.

The hierarchical clustering with a smaller number of variables and cases produced comparable results. The cluster analyses were conducted and cross-validated with samples of 550 cases randomly drawn from the total population of interviewees.

3. The four-cluster solution was considered optimal for several reasons. One, it presented interpretable clusters, each with no more than 33 percent of the cases. Two, the four-cluster solution was readily replicated in subsequent samples, while larger cluster solutions were not. Three, the cluster solutions derived for three through seven clusters produced either excessively large clusters (the three-cluster solution) or very small splinter clusters (the five–seven-cluster solutions) and were less stable than the four-cluster solution. Lastly, the linkage coefficients obtained from the hierarchical cluster analysis suggest that the within-group distances for the five–seven solutions are excessive.

4. The cross-tabulations with the additional abuse and antisocial variables also served to validate the differentiation derived from clustering the weighted scores. The background variables included ordinal responses on age, race, education level, occupation, income, number of children, times married, and length of relationship. The weighted scores of each item used in the cluster analysis were collapsed into proportional categories (low, medium, and high) for convenient comparison.

5. There are of course precautions that must accompany any cluster analysis. The clusters are merely suggestive of the outstanding behavioral differences among the batterers of the Texas shelter women. The findings therefore cannot be used as fixed groupings or diagnostic categories. They are also not meant to suggest a theoretical explanation for battering.

Different algorithms, cluster solutions, or variables often produce different results, and the solutions, as mentioned, are often open to varying interpretations. Moreover, the shelter sample used in this study may overrepresent the more severe batterers and those who have had contact with the police, and underrepresent higher income abusers whose victims are less likely to be in shelters.

6. The typology confirms that the pursuit of a unitary batterer profile is in vain. Much of the current research may have overlooked the diversity of batterers, because it has focused largely on the "sporadic batterer" who becomes apologetic after the abusive incident, as "the cycle of violence" with its honeymoon phase suggests (Walker 1979). These sporadic batterers are likely to have been overrepresented in the studies on batterers, since they are more likely to remain in counseling groups and be receptive to follow-up.

7. There are three additional qualifications that must be made with the police action variable. For one, only the most severe police action is considered in the analysis. The effect of multiple police actions occurring in a case (10 percent of the cases) is not accounted for, although we suspect it is minimal. Two, the measures of abuse do not differentiate between acts related to the police action and those received generally. We can only assume that the most severe abuse and injury is related to the police contact, as other studies suggest (Bowker 1982). Three, even with more sensitive measures for police action, abuse, and background, our discriminant functions account for only a small portion of the variance (20 percent). Perhaps the factors identified here, along with the situational and attitudinal factors identified in previous studies but not researched in this study, would combine to form a more powerful differentiation.

8. Cross-tabulations between representative background and categorical abuse variables and the five major police actions were computed as a preliminary screening

for the multivariate analysis and to develop descriptive data for the police action categories. The full sample of the women who contacted the police was used as the basis for this calculation (n = 3000).

Discriminant functions were used, despite the categorical nature of much of the data, because of the classification rates they offer, which serve as a convenient measure of prediction and allow for the exploratory stepwise analysis presented in table 5–6. Moreover, the findings of the discriminant analysis were supported by the cross-tabulations of table 5–7. Random subsamples of six hundred were used in each discriminant analysis and cross-classification.

6

The Impact of Shelter Services

The most influential help source available to battered women is the shelters from which our sample is drawn. This chapter considers the role of shelters in furthering the helpseeking of battered women. We first summarize the specific kinds of help obtained from shelters and then examine the impact of shelters on the battered women. Our Texas findings, reviewed in the first section of this chapter, suggest that the women's helpseeking is furthered during shelter residence. The discriminant analysis of shelter outcome, discussed in the second section, indicates the importance of providing resources that further independence. It also suggests the need to address the negative effect of batterer counseling on a woman's decision to seek safety.

Helpseeking from Shelters

Shelters for battered women originated as a crisis service and were initially viewed as a help source of last resort. The role of shelters remains primarily to serve as a refuge. According to Bowker and Maurer (1985:6): "Separation, protection, and security are significant in the lives of battered women since they have probably not experienced this degree of personal safety and the opportunity to freely plan their futures since early in their marriage." Many shelters have expanded, as discussed in chapter 1, to include a variety of services that go beyond acting as a refuge and actively assist women to establish more independent lives in the long term. They offer such things as child care, legal assistance, job training, transitional housing, and social service advocacy, as well as supportive counseling or therapy.

The helpseeking of all of our sample, of course, resulted in contacting a local shelter for battered women, since all of the women were shelter residents or nonresidents at the time of the study. As much as 14 percent of our Texas sample had previously contacted a shelter, as indicated in the discussion of previous helpseeking in chapter 3; and as many as 71 percent of the cases had left home previously, however briefly. This compares to the 84 percent of the women in Bowker's (1983) study of formerly abused women who had used shelters in their effort to end the abuse in their relationships.

The helpseeking of the women does not, however, stop with entering a shelter. According to our findings, the shelter women generally seek much more than just refuge. They draw on a large portion of the services provided in a shelter as well as acquire additional resources to help sustain them after leaving the shelter. The shelters appear to play, therefore, a pivotal facilitating role in the continued helpseeking process.

Texas Findings

Shelter Services. A frequency distribution of "shelter services obtained" and "shelter services to be continued" revealed the following about helpseeking from shelters. Once in the shelter, the Texas women drew primarily on the following shelter services: counseling (85 percent), transportation (73 percent), and referral (67 percent) services (see table 6–1). They used an average of 3.3 (s.d. = 2.0) of 7 categories of service; 20 percent used 5 or more different categories of shelter services.

The women when leaving the shelter noted that they would continue to use primarily the crisis hotline (70 percent), counseling (61 percent), and referral services (52 percent) of the shelter (see table 6–2). They mentioned on average two services which they expected to continue ($\bar{x} = 1.7$). About a third of the women said they would continue three or more services. Interestingly, the child, employment, and legal services were less mentioned as services to be continued. This might be because of the increased financial support the women obtained through shelter advocacy or the lack of such services for nonresidents.

Table 6–1
Frequencies for Shelter Services Obtained

	Rank	% of Responses	% of Cases
Category			
Referral	1	20	67
Transportation	2	22	73
Medical care	3	11	37
Child services	4	8	26
Counseling	5	20	86
Legal services	6	7	24
Employment services	7	6	19
Total Mentions $\bar{x} = 3.3$		s.d. = 2.0	
Total Shelter Services Obtained			
Low (1–2)			45
Medium (3–4)			37
High (5–7)			20

Table 6–2
Frequencies for Shelter Services Continued

	Rank	% of Responses	% of Cases
Category			
Information Referral	1	20	52
Legal referral	2	9	23
Transportation	3	4	12
Emergency medical care	4	3	8
Crisis line	5	27	70
Child services	6	7	18
Counseling	7	24	61
Job training	8	6	15
Total Mentions $\bar{x} = 1.7$		s.d. $= 1.9$	
Total Shelter Services Continued			
None			25
Low (1–2)			45
Medium (3–4)			21
High (5–8)			10

The battered women did leave the shelters with varying amounts of resources. These are resources such as personal income, transportation, and child care, which may or may not have been acquired through assistance from the shelter (see table 6–3). Almost half of the women left with some income of their

Table 6–3
Frequencies for Resources Obtained

Variable		Percentage
Own Income (after leaving shelter)		
Own income		49
Job	33	
Public assistance	15	
Not own income		51
Partner	13	
None or undertermined	37	
Own Transportation		
Own car		46
Not own transportation		54
Relative or friend	23	
Public transportation	19	
None	12	
Child Care		
No child care		57
Child care		43
Relative or friend	14	
Babysitter or day care	13	
Care not necessary	23	
Batterer in Counseling		14

own. The number receiving AFDC and spousal income increased during shelter. Forty-six percent of the women indicated that they had their own car. About the same amount (43 percent) had arranged for childcare or did not need it; 13 percent could afford babysitters or day care services.

Living Arrangements. Shelter workers are perhaps most concerned with the living arrangements of the battered women after leaving the shelter, since living separate from the batterer implies greater independence and relative safety. Independent living remains the goal of most shelters, since it has been considered the surest way to end the violence (NiCarthy 1986). The cycle of violence will continue and escalate unless it is decisively interrupted (Walker 1979). Separation in itself, however, does not guarantee safety, since the woman may still be beaten when the batterer comes to visit her or his children (Loseke and Berk 1982). In fact, several shelter assessments indicated that separation did not reduce violence unless it was accompanied by other assistance or interventions (Aguirre 1985; Bowker 1983; Berk et al. 1986).

In our sample, only a quarter (24 percent) of the women planned to return to the batterer, and another quarter (26 percent) planned to live on their own (see table 6–4).[1] Twenty-seven percent planned to live with relatives, 15 percent with friends, and 8 percent were undetermined. This 24 percent return rate upon leaving shelter is less than the 33 percent return rate for a 1980 partial Texas sample (Aguirre 1985) and a Detroit shelter sample (Snyder and Scheer 1981). However, if the "undetermined" category is included as "not returning," the return rate for our sample becomes comparable to the others (31 percent).

The best indication of what actually happens after leaving shelter is the estimates obtained from a survey of some Texas shelter directors and former shelter residents. According to these estimates, 40–50 percent of the residents eventually returned to the batterer (cited in Aguirre 1985). The difficulty in measuring and interpreting actual living arrangements is discussed further below.

Table 6–4
Frequencies for Living Arrangements

Category		Percentage
Return to Batterer		24
Not Return		76
Live with relatives	30	
Live with friends	17	
Client live on own	29	
Total		100

Summary

The Texas shelter women drew on a number of different shelter services, expect to continue using some shelter services after leaving shelter residence, and have obtained resources from other help sources, oftentimes with assistance from the shelter. Obtaining shelter residence, in fact, is more likely a part of a long-term process of helpseeking that may include separating and returning to the batterer several times in the course of ending the violence (Okum 1986).

The actual helpseeking from the shelters is difficult to ascertain, however. This is in part because the services available from or through shelters vary dramatically from shelter to shelter. Some shelters have very elaborate child care programs, some draw on day care programs in the community, and others have little child care available at all. The level of helpseeking from the shelter may therefore be more a reflection of the services available from the shelter, as well as the response of the women to their abuse. There was in fact little correlation between any abuse-related or background variables and the obtained shelter services or shelters services to be continued (Gondolf et al. In press). There is some suggestion, however, that a woman's living arrangements upon leaving the shelter are influenced by the services obtained.

Services and Shelter Outcome

Despite the strong demand for shelter care, there is relatively little research that empirically assesses the impact of shelter services on their residents. The research in this field has been focused primarily on the battered woman and her abuse rather than on her helpseeking and the response of interventions. This is unfortunate for two reasons. One, it has left policymakers with little evidence on which to base their decisions about appropriate intervention (Berk et al. 1986). Two, shelters are left with little evidence of their effectiveness amidst the stiff competition for funds (Bowker and Maurer 1985).

There are a handful of published shelter assessments, however, which do suggest that shelter residence, along with other services, contributes to safer living arrangements. The assessments do not, however, identify the specific kinds of service associated with the outcome. Also, offsetting variables, such as the batterer's being in counseling, have not been sufficiently considered.

We therefore examined the specific services related to a shelter resident's decision whether or not to return to her batterer. According to our findings, variables associated with economic independence, along with the batterer's *not* being in counseling, are the best predictors of a woman's planning to live on her own. Background variables or abuse-related variables do not appear to contribute to the shelter outcome.

Research on Shelter Outcome

The clinical and empirical literature on shelter outcome suggests that about a third of the residents return to their batterer upon leaving the shelter (Aguirre 1985; Martin 1976; Snyder and Scheer 1981; Walker 1979). Several multivariate assessments have attempted to determine why this is so—that is, why women return after initially leaving the batterer and obtaining shelter care. In the process, these assessments have employed varied "predictors" and outcome measures. Outcome has generally been measured in terms of the women's living arrangements after leaving shelter or at some follow-up period. Background, abuse-related, and service-related variables have been considered as predictors. Most of the service-related variables do not, however, specify the kinds of shelter services or other interventions obtained by the woman. The total amount of services or interventions is used instead.

This shortcoming seems especially important to address, given that the specific services, as opposed to background or abuse-related variables, are factors that shelter staff are best equipped to influence. "Specific services" refers here to the kinds of economic and social assistance that a woman has available upon leaving the shelter. These include child care, personal income, transportation, batterer counseling, and legal assistance, as well as continued shelter services.

Outcome Measures. The shelter studies have used the following measures for outcome: the woman's planned living arrangements upon leaving the shelter (Aguirre 1985), her actual living arrangements at some follow-up point (Snyder and Scheer 1981), or the reported level of violence after some follow-up period (Berk et al. 1986). The various findings from these studies suggest, as one might expect, that many women eventually return to their batterer, despite their initial intent to not return.

One follow-up study found, in fact, that while only 14 percent intended to leave the batterer at shelter admission and 33 percent upon leaving shelter, 55 percent of the women were living with the batterer two months after shelter (Snyder and Scheer 1981). Moreover, whether a woman is physically abused or not may not be directly related to her living arrangements; a woman may still be physically abused even if she does separate from the batterer (Berk et al. 1986). An outcome measure for abuse after some extended follow-up period may therefore be the ideal, as Berk et al. (1986) argue.

Our study, nevertheless, uses "planned" living arrangements as a measure of shelter outcome, for these reasons. One, the decision not to return to the batterer appears to have important implications in itself. It is a sign of assertive decision making for women often characterized as beset with learned helplessness (Walker 1979). The mere decision to leave may also afford the battered woman increased leverage with her batterer if she does resume the relationship

(Bowker and Maurer 1985). It is furthermore an important step toward terminating the abusive relationship; it is part of the progressive series of separations and returns in the process of finally separating for good (Okum 1986).

Another reason for using the planned living arrangements as an outcome measure is that it is a more practical measure than follow-up living arrangements or follow-up violence. It is difficult to control for the many extraneous factors related to the ideal follow-up outcome. Also, the cost and difficulty of locating subjects for an extensive follow-up of our sample would make it prohibitive.

Predictors. The previous assessments suggest that the shelter outcome may be best predicted by the degree of economic independence and intervention decisions, along with select background variables. Snyder and Scheer (1981) found the following background variables to be significant predictors in their discriminant function for follow-up living arrangements: length of marriage, occurrence of previous separations, and religious affiliation of the resident (80 percent classification rate).

An assessment considering several abuse-related variables produced negative results, however. Aguirre (1985), using a portion of the Texas intake data from 1980 (n = 1,024), derived a logistic model using variables for no personal income, violence as a child, number of issues related to battering, and number of injuries from abuse. Only "husband as sole source of income" was statistically significant.

The limited use of service-related predictors suggests that the extent of shelter service coupled with other interventions, like obtaining legal assistance or court injunction, is also important. Aguirre (1985), in another part of her study, examined the influence of several service-related variables: number of intervention decisions made during shelter stay, number of shelter services used, client's evaluation of the shelter, and whether the batterer was in counseling. The "number of decisions" was the only variable that proved to be statistically significant; "batterer in counseling" and "positive evaluation of the shelter" were both positively associated with a return to the batterer, even though not significant.[2] Berk et al. (1986), with the most sophisticated analysis thus far, demonstrated further the interactive effect of shelter stay and other interventions in reducing the number of violences.[3] According to their logistic findings, the effects of shelter care appear to be related to a woman's actively taking control of her life.

Method

Hypothesis. Our research attempted to extend and clarify the previous shelter assessments by introducing variables which specify the economic independence and intervention decisions shown to be influential in shelter outcome. We expected that the women discharged from shelter would be more likely not to return to their batterers if they had acquired their own income, transportation, and child care, and thus have lessened their dependence on their batterer. Their tendency to separate would also be influenced by interventions, like legal assistance and calling the police, that is, interventions which suggest to the batterer that the woman "means business." Initially, we did not expect the batterer's being in counseling to be particularly influential.

Variables. Our outcome measure, as mentioned above, was "planned living arrangements"—the client's decision upon leaving shelter to return to the batterer or not return to him. (The 8 percent of the total sample who indicated that they were "undetermined" with regard to living arrangements were deleted from the analysis.)

The predictor variables include service-related variables associated with economic independence, intervention decisions, and shelter service. Three dichotomous (yes/no) variables were used to operationalize economic independence: the woman's having her "own income," "own transportation," and "child care" upon leaving the shelter. Three additional dichotomous variables were used to operationalize intervention decisions: "legal assistance sought during shelter," "previous contact with the police," and "batterer in counseling." Shelter services were measured as the "total number of shelter services obtained" and the "total number of services to be continued after leaving shelter."

Lastly, twenty-four background and abuse-related variables ("actuarial" variables) were selected from the shelter intake interview (see table 6–6 for the full listing).[4]

Analysis. A series of stepwise discriminant functions were used to investigate the relationship of the service-related variables to outcome.[5] First, a discriminant function was computed for the eight service-related variables to determine their influence as predictors. Second, a function was computed for the service-related variables and twenty-four actuarial variables. This operation was used to ascertain whether actuarial variables could substantially enhance or supersede the service-related variables as predictors.[6]

Findings

The discriminant function for the eight service-related variables showed that batterer in counseling (−.57), along with own transportation (.50), child care (.49), and own income (.31) are the most influential predictors of shelter outcome. Whereas, the other intervention and total services variables have little or no predictive power (see table 6–5). Moreover, the inclusion of the actuarial variables in the discriminant analysis did not increase the classification rate (79 percent).[7] In fact, the batterer-in-counseling and independence variables remained predominant in the function (see table 6–6). Those background

Table 6–5
Stepwise Discriminant Function
of Service-Related Variables
(8 variables entered)

Predictor	Disc. Coeff.
Batterer in counseling*	− .57
Own transportation*	.50
Child care*	.49
Own income*	.31
Legal assistance through shelter*	.11
Services continued after leaving shelter	.11

Not Significant: Shelter services obtained,
Police contacted*.

Eigenvalue = .19; Canonical Corr. = .40; Lambda
= .84; χ^2 = 103.18 (6); p < .00001; Correct
classification = 79% (n = 500)

*Dichotomous variable.

variables related to class and those related to physical abuse were not significant, contrary to Gelles's (1976) hypothesis. We might assume, therefore, that the service-related variables are relatively sufficient in themselves for predicting shelter outcome.

Cross-tabulations of batterer in counseling with planned living arrangements (the shelter outcome measure) further illustrate the strong influence of this particular predictor. Nineteen percent of the women *without* batterers in counseling planned to return to their batterers, as opposed to 53 percent of the women *with* batterers in counseling—almost three times the proportion (see table 6–7). The overriding effect of batterer counseling is evident in the cross-tabulations controlling for income. Only 16 percent of the women *with an income* returned to their batterers, while as much as 38 percent of the women *with an income* were planning to return to the batterer if he was *in counseling* (X^2 = 18.68(1); $p \leq$ .00001). Controlling for "violence against others" or "previously arrested" did not appreciably alter the "return" percentage for the batterer-in-counseling variable.

Implications

Our study of shelter outcome offers three major findings: the predominant influence of batter in counseling, the influence of economic independence, and the lack of influence of the background and abuse variables. The study appears to imply the importance of shelters' providing additional resources for their residents and also monitoring the services of batterers. To accomplish this end, community services in general need to be better coordinated.

Table 6–6
Stepwise Discriminant Function of Background, Abuse, and Service-Related Variables
(32 variables entered)

Predictors	Disc. Coeff.
Batterer in counseling*	− .54
Own transportation*	.44
Child care*	.44
Own income source after shelter*	.33
Emergency room care*	.29
Batterer threatened to harm child*	.27
Verbal abuse	− .25
Witnessed abuse as child	.24
Weapons used*	− .21
Shelter services continued	.15
Child abuse*	.15
Batterer threaten to kill*	.15
Racial minority*	− .13
Police contacted*	− .11
Alcohol abuse related to abuse*	− .11
Income amount prior to shelter	− .11

Not Significant: Shelter services obtained, Legal assistance, Woman's age, Woman's income amount, Woman's education, Number of children, Physical abuse, Abused in previous relationship*, Frequency of abuse, Duration of abuse, Injuries, Broken bones*, Total issues related to abuse, General violence, Batterer employed*, Batterer arrested*, Previous helpseeking.

Eigenvalue = .30; Canonical Corr. = .48; Lambda = .77; χ^2 = 125.52 (16); p < .00001; Correct classification = 79% (n = 500)

*Dichotomous variable.

Economic Independence. The three service variables associated with independence, along with the batterer's not being in counseling, were the best predictors of a woman's not returning to her batterer. These findings bear out the previous research indicating the importance of economic independence in separating from the batterer (Aguirre 1985; Strube and Barbour 1983). Services that specifically assure personal income, transportation, and child care appear to have an impact on living arrangements and therefore need to accompany shelter refuge. In other words, making resources available seems to make a difference.

The importance of intervention decisions, suggested by Aguirre (1985) and Berk et al. (1986) is somewhat contradicted, however. Furthermore, the total of shelter services does not appear to be influential in itself, as Aguirre (1985) previously showed. It may be that our intervention variables need to consider more the nature or quality of the intervention or services. Also, the range of

Table 6–7
Cross-Tabulation of Living Arrangements
by Batterer-in-Counseling

Living Arrangements	Batterer in Counseling		Total
	No	Yes	
Return to batterer	19%	53%	24%
Not return	81	47	76
	84	16	100

$\chi^2 = 85.17$ (1); $p < .00001$ (n = 1000)

available services could vary from shelter to shelter in a way that negates their influence as a predictor variable.

Batterer Counseling. One outstanding finding nevertheless remains—that is, the inordinate influence that the batterer's counseling has on the women's decision to return to the relationship.[8] The influence of batterer's counseling raises important theoretical and programmatic implications. In terms of theory, this finding supports the hypothesis that women stay in abusive relationships because they expect that their batterer will change (Frieze 1979; Pfouts 1978). In fact, nearly three-quarters (73 percent) of one shelter sample reportedly returned because "the batterer repented" or "they believed he would change" (Pagelow 1981). Batterer counseling, most probably, offers the hope that "this time he *is* really going to change," and thus makes returning to the batterer a rational option in many women's minds.

Unfortunately, batterers often use counseling as a form of manipulation rather than as a means of change. As many clinical studies observe, most batterers initially attend counseling to get their wives back, dropping out as soon as the threat of separation is over (see Gondolf 1985). The high drop-out and recidivism rates appear to bear this out (Priog–Good and Stets–Kealey 1986).

There are two further problems with the association between batterer counseling and "returning." One, counseling programs vary widely and many are simply not equipped to deal with the serious nature of abuse, and therefore present false hopes. Two, as discussed in chapter 5, nearly a third of the batterers of shelter women may be considered severely antisocial men who are likely to be unresponsive to counseling (Gondolf 1987b).

The programmatic implication is that shelter services are likely to be offset by batterer counseling.[9] That is, even after provision of child care, personal income, or transportation, a woman is likely to be drawn back to her batterer by the fact that he is in counseling. Shelter staff, therefore, need to better apprise the women of the limitations of batterer counseling. Moreover, it is obviously in their interest to closely monitor batterer programs. In light of these findings, it may even be their right to supervise counseling programs, given the tremendous influence they have on the women's decisions (see Hart 1987).

Coordinating Services. In sum, the resources obtained by women during shelter are important to gaining safety. As several studies have argued, the increased economic independence of battered women enables women to leave their battering husbands. This is a particularly crucial matter, given the low economic status of a substantial portion of the shelter women, as discussed in chapter 4. In fact, one prominent study suggests that greater women's equality reflected in women's incomes, educational levels, and legal rights may be a deterrent to wife abuse (Yllo 1983). States with the greatest "equality" tend to have less wife abuse.

Admittedly, leaving the batterer is more complicated than simply having a way out. Our findings also indicate that the batterer's being in counseling is one such compounding factor. The kind of encouragement, programming, and counseling received by a battered woman while residing in a shelter is no doubt a factor too. Those factors aside, the women, when given a clear opportunity to separate from the batterer, tend to do so.

The overall implication in these findings is that shelters cannot do it alone. More than shelter refuge is needed to help women maintain some semblance of safety. Battered women need a wide variety of services and resources to leave their batterers. There also needs to be vigilant coordination with batterer programs to assure that the batterer's counseling does not mistakenly lure women back to an unsafe relationship. In sum, the community help sources need to be more systematically coordinated in order to effectively assist wife abuse. As will be discussed further in the concluding chapter, the active helpseeking of battered women—before, during, and after shelter—needs to be met with more generous helpgiving.

Notes

1. Eighty-nine percent of the women were living with the batterer at the time of intake.

2. Okum (1986), in a bivariate analysis, did find that 83 percent of the batterers in counseling with a shelter-related batterers' program resumed living with their wives, and 65 percent of the batterers not entering counseling returned to their wives within one year of their leaving shelter.

3. Berk et al. (1986) developed a logistic regression for reduced violences using shelter or prosecutor cases. Their covariates included a "propensity score" that controls for treatment effects. "Days at risk" and previous helpseeking were also controlled. Their outcome measure is the only one to consider the recurrences of violence at follow-up, instead of living arrangements.

4. The logrithmic transformations of some of these variables were used in the analysis in order to approximate a normal distribution.

5. As in the previous chapters, discriminant functions were used in the analysis, despite the categorical nature of the data; because of the classification rates, they offer a convenient measure of prediction and allow for the exploratory stepwise analysis presented in table 6–6. Moreover, the findings of the discriminant analysis of table 6–5 were replicated in a logistic regression.

6. Random subsamples of 800 were used in the discriminant computation and in cross-classification tests. Also, the service variables were cross-tabulated with outcome (n = 1,000) to describe further the influence of the predictors.

7. This classification rate is comparable to that derived from a discriminant function for a series of background variables (80 percent) (Snyder and Scheer 1981).

8. As mentioned, batter in counseling was not statistically significant in Aguirre's (1986) multivariate study of the 1980 partial Texas sample. This may be a reflection of the relatively few counseling programs available at the time of this particular sample.

9. These implications deserve particular attention, given the advent of court-mandated counseling for batterers.

Table 7–1
A Summary of the Study Findings

1. *The women in the Texas shelters have experienced extremely severe levels of abuse; more severe than that reported by samples of battered women from other states.* Over 40 percent of the Texas women had been abused with weapons; over two-thirds had their lives verbally threatened. Sixty percent had been kicked, and over one-fourth had been sexually abused. Also, the children of nearly half of the women with children had been physically abused. The wife abuse resulted in head injuries for half of the women, broken bones for 13 percent, and hospitalization for 10 percent. Moreover, the abuse had been occurring weekly for nearly half of the women, and for a year or more in two-thirds of the cases. (See chapter 1.)

2. *The battered women suffer from additional problems that make their recovery and safety more difficult to achieve.* A substantial portion live in poverty, have little education, and have generally "antisocial" batterers. Specifically, over half of the women have no personal income of their own; less than 6 percent are on welfare. Half of the women have less than a high school education. Three-fourths of their husbands make under $15,000 a year, and nearly a third are unemployed. Less than 60 percent of the women are white. Moreover, most of the women (60 percent) are married to men who abuse alcohol. Half of the alcohol abusers have been arrested for drunk driving and 70 percent also use drugs. Nearly 60 percent of all the men had been arrested for some offense, and 40 percent are violent outside the family. (See chapter 1.)

3. *The battered women appear more as "survivors" than as victims of "learned helplessness."* They have actively tried to get help; in fact, they have contacted on average five different kinds of helping sources. Over half of the women had contacted the police, and 20 percent had previously sought legal assistance prior to becoming a shelter resident. Nearly a third of the women had visited an emergency room at some time. Moreover, the more severe the abuse and antisocial behavior (substance abuse, arrests, and general violence) from the batterer, the more different help sources were contacted. The abuse that women experienced as a child and other background variables do not appear to significantly influence her helpseeking. (See chapter 3.)

4. *There are differences between residents and nonresidents and among racial groups that may warrant different kinds of services.* Women receiving nonresident services tend to be from higher socioeconomic status, have been victims of less frequent abuse, and have less generally violent batterers. White, black, and Hispanic resident women have experienced similar levels of abuse. However, the Hispanic women have much lower educational and economic status than the black and white women. They generally have more children and have endured the abuse for a longer period of time. (See chapter 4.)

5. *The batterers may be categorized by their abuse and antisocial behavior; this categorization suggests that the same intervention may not be appropriate for all batterers.* Over 30 percent of the batterers could be characterized as sociopathic or antisocial batterers who are violent to nonfamily members, have criminal records, and heavily abuse drugs and alcohol, as well as being severely abusive to their wives and children. Only about 30 percent of the batterers appear to be sporadic abusers who are generally apologetic, as the "cycle of violence" with the honeymoon phase suggests. The antisocial batterers are just as likely to be in counseling as the chronic and sporadic batterers who are not generally violent outside the home (14 percent). The sociopathic and antisocial batterers are more likely to be in counseling because of court mandate, and the sporadic batterers are more likely to be self-referred and more responsive to treatment. (See chapter 5.)

6. *Police appear to be responding more to antisocial men than to the wife abuse itself.* The more antisocial the batterer, the more likely he is to get arrested (15 percent of all batterers). However, nearly 20 percent of the women who contacted the police were severely abused but by less antisocial batterers, and therefore received "no action" from the police. Interestingly, nearly half of the women offered a positive appraisal of the police; but the lower income women were more likely to have a positive appraisal than the higher income women. (See chapter 5.)

7
Summary and Recommendations

This final chapter begins with a summary of our research findings and follows with recommendations for shelter programs, social services, and policymakers. The study summary, in particular, notes the apparent neglect of women who are for the most part severely terrorized by abuse and trapped in poverty. The recommendations specifically address means of increasing responsiveness and particularly the resources allocated to these women. Several models for integrating community services to address wife abuse are presented. We conclude with an appeal to "treat" the learned helplessness within the help sources that should be helping more.

Study Summary

The Helpseeking

Our study of battered women in Texas shelters produced several major empirical findings:

1. The helpseeking behavior of battered women is diverse and extensive.
2. Life-threatening abuse is compounded by severe poverty and lack of resources.
3. A substantial portion of "antisocial" batterers are unlikely to be responsive to batterer counseling.
4. Additional resources are vital in enabling separation from the batterer (see table 7–1).

The most outstanding of these findings is that the battered women are active helpseekers. The women's helpseeking appears to increase as the batterer becomes more apparently dangerous and incorrigible. The women, in sum, are not the passive victims that notions of learned helplessness would imply.

Table 7–1 continued

7. *Shelter advocacy appears to have an impact on the women's move toward safety.* Only 25 percent of the women planned to return to the batterer upon leaving the shelter. The women are more likely *not* to return to the batterer if they have child care, transportation, and income available and have obtained a variety of shelter services. The women with batterers in counseling are the ones most likely to return to the batterer upon leaving the shelter. The women's background or previous abuse does not substantially influence their living arrangements. (See chapter 6.)

They are in fact "survivors," in that they assertively and persistently attempt to do something about their abuse. They contact a variety of help sources where one would expect to find assistance. The help sources, however, do not appear to muster the decisive intervention necessary to stop the cycle of violence.

Our findings suggest, moreover, that this level of helpseeking is relatively constant among white, Hispanic, and black women, and among various income levels. The severity and kind of abuse is also comparable among these groupings. One must not infer, however, that all of these groups should be treated the same. There are some clear background differences that warrant differentiated help.

For one, the Hispanic women bear an extra burden of lower income, less education, and more children, as well as cultural and language differences. Moreover, the undocumented status of a substantial portion of the Hispanic women makes it difficult for them to obtain needed services. Interestingly, the economic and educational status of the white and black shelter residents is not that different, although discrimination experienced by the black women no doubt constitutes another obstacle to their achieving safety and independence.

Two, we found a higher economic class of women obtaining shelter care as nonresidents. These nonresident women appear to warrant more formalized support services than the shelter residents, because of their class-based expectations, available resources, and relative mobility. Nonresident services, in this light, are reaching a category of battered women who have been less likely to seek shelter residence. The services may, therefore, be preventing the escalation of violence that might otherwise result.

The Reign of Terror

Probably the most alarming facts concerning the Texas women are the most obvious and well known. These women have been seriously, frequently, and persistently abused. The shelter women, in general, are clearly not avoiding the responsibilities of marriage, seeking a handout, or escaping from family squabbles, as some New Right proponents would suggest. A substantial portion have had weapons used against them (43 percent), had threats made against their lives (70 percent), and required emergency room care (31 percent). And for nearly two-thirds of the women, this abuse has continued for a year or more.

The abuse statistics become even more alarming when we attempt to comprehend the composite of these various measures. As Walker (1984) has noted in her research, there is inevitably a "chaining" effect that occurs in abuse. The hits, shoves, and verbal put-downs are not experienced by the women as the separate acts identified by researchers. They serve to instate the man's control, domination, and privilege. Moreover, this cumulative impact should be interpreted as part of a larger context of past abuse, personal background, and community response.

When we consider the range of physical and verbal abuses, and their frequent context of poverty and unresponsive services, as a unified phenomenon, the abuse events merge into a reign of terror. The battered women are subjected to the constant possibility of being attacked and injured by their batterers, with no escape or aid. Moreover, like those living in the war-torn city of Beirut, the women have little recourse or chance of escape. Yet these women, despite the odds against them, have sought some means of ending the violence.

The other alarming fact apparent in this study of shelter women is the dire economic status of these abused women. Well over half (58 percent) of the women have no personal income and no high school diploma. Even with the income of their batterers, the majority of the women's families are living below the poverty line. And in the entire Texas sample, nearly a third are black or Hispanic.

These conditions are in themselves evidence of a public form of abuse that compounds the family abuse. They reflect, no doubt, what several social scientists have identified as "the feminization of poverty." That is, an increasing proportion of those living in poverty are women and children.

The coincidence of severe abuse and severe poverty in so many shelter women raises some harsh issues. Can shelters effectively assist these women by providing primarily shelter and advocacy, as they have in the past? Shelters, like it or not, are becoming modern-day poorhouses. Their residents not only need a haven from abuse; they also need resources to support themselves. If there is not a sound bridge out of the poverty, there is little reason to suspect that the women can afford to live separate from the batterer.

Antisocial Batterers

Our research also examined the nature of the batterer and found, in the process, yet another difficulty adding to the abuse itself. A substantial portion of the men could be typified as having previous arrests, being violent to more than the battered women, and severely abusing alcohol and drugs. Many of the shelter women were, therefore, contending not only with abusers but also with seriously antisocial and even sociopathic individuals.

Our typology of the men, based on their behavior as reported by the women, appears to cut across class and racial lines. The types include sporadic, chronic, antisocial, and sociopathic batterers. The sporadic batterers were the only type that appeared to conform to the "cycle of violence" notion. That is, they characteristically lapsed into an apologetic "honeymoon" phase after being physically abusive. The other types of batterers were just as likely to deny the abuse or threaten to do it again.

These findings raise serious issues about intervention. For one, they suggest that arrest for abuse may not be sufficient for the type of men who have repeatedly had previous contact with the law and not been deterred from repeating violence or other unlawful behavior. Two, there appears to be at least a portion of what we termed "sociopathic" batterers who may need intensive psychiatric treatment as well as restraint.

Three, the findings suggest that the majority of men are not likely to be responsive to batterer counseling programs, given the complexity of their problems. Anger control treatment, which is widely used in batterer programs, may be applicable only to the sporadic batterers and a portion of the chronic batterers. This is a particularly crucial matter since an equal portion (14 percent) of each type of batterer was found to be in counseling, and the women were most likely to return to the batterer if he was in counseling. In short, many women return to men in counseling who are highly likely to repeat their abuse and intensify it.

Moreover, police action appears to be a useful but limited intervention with the batterers. Over half the shelter women had previously contacted the police, but only 15 percent of the cases resulted in an arrest and 32 percent resulted in the police "doing nothing." Our analysis suggests, in fact, that the police are more likely to take action against the batterer if the man is generally antisocial in his behavior—that is, an abuser of alcohol and drugs, previously arrested, generally violent, and verbally abusive. The police appear to be more intent on "handling" antisocial men than addressing the wife abuse. Consequently, a substantial portion of severely abused women with less antisocial men receive inadequate police response.

Resource Allocation

Lastly, we found, consistent with our survivor hypothesis, that battered women are inclined to leave their batterers, if they are provided the resources to do so. In other words, resource allocation makes a difference. The women who have transportation, child care, and their own source of income upon leaving the shelter are more likely to live separate from the batterer. The amount of shelter services or counseling received, as well as the women's background or abuse severity, do not appear to be influential factors in their choice of living arrangements. In fact, only a quarter of the shelter women planned to return to the batterer upon shelter exit. This in itself verifies the women's determination to escape the batterer and courage to brave it on their own.

The most influential predictor of a woman's return to the batterer, as mentioned, is the batterer's being in counseling. The women were over twice as likely to return to the batterer if he was in counseling. This finding reinforces the speculation that women return to the batterer because they think he is going to change. Being in a counseling program apparently suggests to the women that the batterer is trying to change. The reality may be, given our typology of batterers, that most of these men are not likely to change through counseling alone, and may be using the counseling to manipulate the women or appease authorities. The only assurance of change for many men may be in their long-term involvement in a highly restrictive residential program that treats their antisocial, mental health, and substance abuse problems along with their abuse of their wives.

In sum, shelter women need access to more resources to enable their separation from the batterer, at least during his incarceration or treatment. And batterers need to be subjected to intensive and extensive programming that addresses their abuse and multiple problems of a distorted masculinity. These needs are particularly important given the trend toward poorer and more severely abused women in shelters.

Recommendations

Expanding Shelter Programs

We have discussed specific implications for shelters at the end of each chapter. Rather than repeat them here, we offer instead a more general conception of the objectives for shelters in light of the overall findings. Basically, our findings support the initial conception of shelters as a haven that provides battered women a temporary residence and supportive environment.

As Bowker's (1983) evaluative study of help sources indicates, shelters are considered by battered women to be the most effective of all the services contacted. The women note their appreciation of the supportive counseling and the advocacy in shelters, as opposed to the more directive therapy and bureaucracy of traditional agencies.

Shelters also generally provide some essential basics: a safe place from the abuse, time to recover from emotional and physical hurts, and a supportive environment to reassess their situation and options. As many in the shelter movement have pointed out, the most important contribution may be that shelter residence breaks down the isolation most battered women have experienced. Learning that they are not alone reinforces the realization that it is not "just them."

Our evidence confirms, furthermore, that shelters are an important reinforcement for the helpseeking of battered women. The shelters appear to act as a transition place for women already in the process of helpseeking. They demonstrate that at least some helpseeking efforts can be worthwhile and effective. The shelters can also help escalate helpseeking through referral and advocacy that lead women to other help sources, such as job training, public assistance, child care, and legal aid. Lastly, the shelters give leverage to the woman who does return to her batterer. It conveys that the woman means business and has someone to back her up.

As Bowker and Maurer (1985) argue in their comparison of shelters to traditional agencies, this is all accomplished in a relatively unsophisticated communal setting with paraprofessionals and volunteers as primary service providers. Shelters are therefore highly cost effective. The negotiating of daily tasks, like meal preparation and child supervision, provides practice in reorienting one's life, as well as informal support and friendship. The flexible and informal structure of most shelters also allows women to work through their hurts at their own pace and in their own way, rather than face the rigid standards and procedures of some masculinized professional services.

This does not mean that shelter life is all peaches and cream. At times it may be a highly volatile and chaotic environment. Women fearing reprisals, facing impoverishment, with restless children, and having different backgrounds are all confined to very tight quarters. Furthermore, staff are overworked and short of resources. Troubled or criminal women occasionally undermine the unity, as well. Some decisive rules, assertive administration, case management, and a well-trained and compensated staff are needed to offset these problems.

Also, it is clear from our findings that the shelters cannot do it alone. Most of the women face multiple challenges, like little income and education, which cannot be redressed by shelter service. A wide range of services and supports are needed for women to achieve autonomous living, and most of those are not readily available. Many women, therefore, return to the batterer as a necessary means of coping with their circumstances.

Obtaining Additional Services

The communal experience of a well-managed shelter is not sufficient in and of itself. In fact, the shelter work can be severely frustrating and unsatisfying if there are not additional resources or support services to meet the survival needs of the shelter women. As our results attest, the women need tremendous financial and legal assistance. They need child care and parenting aid. They need housing, transportation, and further protection. These additional services may be provided through one of several delivery models (see table 7–2).

Shelter Advocacy. The predominant model for additional services is the shelter referral or advocacy approach. In this approach, shelter staff put battered women

Table 7–2
Models for Increasing Service Delivery

Shelter Advocacy: Shelters provide a safe transitional residence with communal living arrangements. Additional resources and support services are obtained through shelter referral to community agencies and advocacy, especially with the criminal justice system.

Shelter–Agency Priority: Shelters additionally allocate specialized agency services through vouchers or priority status for battered women. Services such as child care, job training, transportation, low-income housing are obtained directly from agencies without bureaucratic red tape or protracted advocacy.

Shelter Clearinghouse: A separate office maintains case management of abused women and coordinates especially the interventions of law enforcement and social services for reported domestic violence cases. For instance, at police contact a battered women is referred to a shelter, legal assistance, and child services, and receives assistance in obtaining the service she needs.

Integrated Interventions: Domestic violence program directs a system of prescribed interventions that may be contracted from various agencies but are prescribed as part of a sequential whole. For instance, an abused women may receive support counseling, shelter care, transitional housing, follow-up support, and job training while her batterer passes through a similar sequence of extended interventions.

in contact with other community agencies that provide services the women need. But in many cases, this amounts to passing women to other agencies ill-equipped to deal with the urgency of their needs. Consequently, some shelters have managed to establish vouchers or priority status for shelter women to obtain child care, job training, and housing. Others have expanded into multiservice centers with in-house job training, legal assistance, and day care programs. The Austin, Texas, shelter has pioneered a transitional housing program that allows shelter women to move into long-term housing rentals managed by the shelter (U.S. Department of Housing and Urban Development, 1987). The expansion of nonresident programs has also offered another alternative for women with their own housing.

The advantage to the multiservice approach is that resource allocation is readily coordinated and assured by the shelter. The main shortcoming is that this approach may stretch shelter finances and lead to a specialized staffing structure. As some shelter directors have noted, the multiservice approach puts them in the position of delivering service that should be taken care of by other agencies in the community. The shelters end up doing other agencies' work for them, when they have plenty to do themselves.

Coordinated Community Services. Another option is for shelters to work in a coalition with a coordinated system of community services. A few model community programs, like the Domestic Abuse Project in Minneapolis, maintain a central clearinghouse for all wife abuse cases (Brygger and Edleson 1987). This assures that battered women who have contact with any social or law enforcement agency will also receive direct referral to other needed services. The batterer, as well, is directed to a treatment program or possibly arrested.

The crucial question becomes: how community services might be made more responsive to battered women, let alone made to participate in some co-ordinated effort? Our study suggests that such services, for the most part, have been ineffective in stopping abuse. Numerous studies have, in fact, verified the shortcomings of community services in dealing with abuse. Some agency staff question the paraprofessional or feminist orientation of shelters, others avoid wife battering cases because of sexism or personal anxiety about the issue, and others are simply inadequate to address abuse cases when they do identify them.

Treating Social Services

Helplessness in Social Services. While there are claims of sexism and systematic neglect, there is, we believe, a more fundamental problem to be addressed—that of learned helplessness among the social services. Service staff face the "uncontrollable" environment, noted by the proponents of learned helplessness, in terms of unchanged clients, overwhelming caseloads, and insufficient resources. Moreover, they have no compelling motivation to draw on some survivor instinct to halt learned helplessness, because most of their jobs are assured despite their work conditions.

But the situation of wife abuse also presents a troublesome aspect in itself. It does not "fit" the design of the crisis orientation and specialized format of most established community interventions and services. It is in fact a long-term chronic problem that requires long-term intervention and support, rather than crisis intervention and piecemeal services. Abuse does not, moreover, conform to a neat category like theft, unemployment, or mental illness. It often includes aspects of all of these as well as a state of terror and oppression all its own. As numerous studies have shown, most social services, mental health agencies, emergency rooms, and law enforcement agents end up dealing with only the immediate symptoms of abuse.

Help sources are, in sum, simply not equipped to deal effectively with abuse and therefore are bound to encounter frustration and discouragement if and when they do attempt to deal with it. There are of course many services that are overwhelmed in treating their own specialized populations. They are therefore inclined to dismiss or avoid abuse cases. What, for instance, does a poverty agency facing countless homeless families do in the case of the middle-class battered woman who has recently become impoverished because she has fled her husband and home for safety?

Improving Service Delivery. The conditions underlying the learned helplessness of social services must ultimately be addressed. It means that services and interventions need to be integrated in a fashion that fits the abuse cases. As in treatments for other forms of learned helplessness, the environment has to be made more manageable and one's ability to affect it more apparent. The service delivery models outlined above can go a long way in accomplishing this.

Improved referral and advocacy can bring better and more services to the battered woman. The ideal would be that the woman's contact with any help source promptly activates referral to a variety of services. This in itself would begin to offset the piecemeal responses which are by themselves doomed to failure. Similarly, the priority allocation of services, like child care for battered women, would begin to expand the narrow specializations that preclude response to the battered woman.

Service coordination through a clearinghouse system, as discussed above, might offer a more appropriate and efficient use of existing services, one that assures the simultaneous use of a variety of services and feedback between them. Simply having the battered woman and batterer in collaborative programs at the same time would no doubt improve effectiveness and decrease the chance of contradictions in approaches or lapses in safety.

The ideal, we believe, is to establish a unified program of integrated interventions that is tailored to the battered woman and batterer. This would amount to a phased set of interventions tailored to the recovery processes in the man and woman (Gondolf 1987c). Abuse as a phenomenon would be dealt with comprehensively and directly, thus increasing effectiveness and reducing frustration of both the victim and service provider.

Policy Innovations

Government Initiative. The improvement of social service delivery, however, cannot be brought about solely at the local level. It requires extensive support, funding, and legislation at the state and national levels in order to become a reality. Given the inertia of laissez-faire attitudes, fiscal conservatism, and pro-family platforms, a strong federal government program is required, just as it was in the attack on segregation and more recently on drug abuse. But as with many social problems, improved policy and intervention will actually reduce costs in the long run.

For one, effective intervention will release the potential of thousands of women who have previously expended all their energies on surviving abuse. Many of these formerly battered women have already more than repaid the costs of their sheltering by working as volunteers and paraprofessionals in the shelter movement. Other battered women have moved on to gain education and jobs that make them contributing citizens of the community. Two, effective intervention also avoids tremendous future costs for treating the children disturbed by growing up in an abusive household and for dealing with their eventual families where abuse is likely to be reenacted.

The government initiative might support the local efforts to improve service delivery to battered women in the following ways: expanded funding of social services for women, legislation that promotes decisive and extended intervention, programs that address the feminization of poverty, and more comprehensive treatments for male violence (see table 7–3).

Many in the shelter movement have been fighting for such initiatives for years and made some substantial gains. Monies for shelters have held relatively steady amidst government cutbacks, even though they need to be substantially

Table 7–3
Policy Recommendations for Stopping Wife Abuse

Expanded Shelter Funding: Funding that provides for expansion of shelters to accommodate more women and children and allows for short-term and long-term shelter. Shelter staffs need to be expanded, and salaries raised to attract and hold competent workers, as is the much-publicized case with teaching positions.

Earmarked Resources: Funding allocations to establish priority resources for abused women and their children. Special child-care services and transitional housing allotments for battered women need to be made available, much as there are earmarked allotments for some minority groups or the elderly in some service delivery. Special programming for children of abusive families is also needed.

Coordinated Interventions: Government support for developing and managing a better coordination of existing services. Services must be coordinated in a systematic way to address the multiple needs, much as service systems have been devised to address the chronically mentally ill.

"Say No" Publicity: A national-level campaign to establish that abuse of any kind is unacceptable and has severe consequences. Advertising would follow much the approach of the antidrug campaign being conducted nationwide.

Pro-Intervention Laws: Legislation that assures prompt investigation and decisive intervention into suspected wife abuse cases. Statutes would require the reporting of suspected wife abuse, much as is currently done in the case of suspected child abuse. Also, accountability of law enforcement agencies is need to assure that such legislation is implemented.

Antipoverty Programs: Extended programming to assure job training and employment for low-income individuals in general, and especially for battered women. Some of the current welfare reform proposals provide for such a similar workfare plan to be accompanied by child-care services.

Women's Rights: Legislation on the order of the civil rights lawmaking of the sixties that furthers women's rights, especially in divorce, employment, and abuse situations. Abused women, for instance, need to be guaranteed adequate alimony and child support.

Male Violence Prevention: Nonviolence and relationship education that teaches males alternatives to the masculine cultural norms of aggression, competition, and exploitation. Courses could be instituted in schools for young men and at mental health centers for adults much like sex education or birthing classes are conducted.

Long-Term Batterer Treatment: Phased programs for batterers that progress from jailing to educational programs to self-help support to community service, much life the Alcoholics Anonymous scheme. Also, intensive residential programs for multiple-problem men, much like a "detoxification" center or model residential programs for rapists.

increased. Legislation criminalizing domestic violence and allowing for "probable cause" arrests now exists in many states. The number of treatment programs for men who batter, including court-mandated counseling, has also increased.

Specific Recommendations. As our study suggests, however, serious deficiencies remain. In fact, all of these areas of accomplishment need to be expanded and implemented more broadly. There are several specific initiatives that might serve to remedy the shortfalls that we have identified. All of these have precedent in other fields and have been shown to be feasible and relatively effective.

First, social services might be extended by funding for expanding shelter facilities and staff salaries, earmarking resources for battered women, and development of coordinated interventions. Expanded shelter funding might provide for expansion of shelters to accommodate more women and children and allow for short-term and long-term shelter. Shelter staffs also need to be expanded, and salaries raised to attract and hold competent workers, as is the much publicized case with teaching positions in our schools. Furthermore, support of paraprofessional positions could provide employment for more women in the community, as well as for more formerly battered women who are interested in assisting at a shelter.

Funding allocations to establish priority resources for abused women are also essential. Special child-care services and transitional housing allotments for battered women need to be made available, much as there are earmarked allotments for some minority groups or the elderly in some service delivery systems. Programming to help the children who have witnessed or experienced violence also needs to be made available in and after shelter. These children need assistance in recovering from the trauma of abuse and adjusting to a new life, in order to avoid reenacting the abuse in their adult life. Special programs for children of alcoholics offer a model in this regard.

There should be, moreover, government support for developing and managing a better coordination of existing services. Services must be coordinated in a systematic way to address the multiple needs, much as service systems have been devised to address the chronically mentally ill.

Second, government initiative needs to include legislation that promotes decisive and extended intervention. A national-level campaign is needed to more emphatically establish that abuse of any kind is unacceptable and has severe consequences. Anti-abuse advertising might follow the approach of the anti-drug campaign: "Just Say No."

Legislation must also assure prompt and decisive investigation into suspected wife abuse cases. Statutes should require the reporting of suspected wife abuse, much as is currently done in the case of suspected child abuse. In this way, service responsiveness might be enhanced and the escalation of violence abated. Such legislation is of little effect, however, unless implementation by police and district attorneys is assured through greater accountability of law enforcement agencies.

Antipoverty programs targeted at women need to be in place as well. Shelter women are especially in need of job training and employment programs, as are women in general. Some of the current welfare reform proposals provide, for example, a workfare plan to be accompanied by expanded child-care services.

As the women's movement has advocated, legislation on the order of the civil rights lawmaking of the sixties is needed to further women's rights, especially in divorce, employment, and abuse situations. Abused women, for instance, need to be guaranteed adequate alimony and child support.

A third area in need of government support is establishment of more comprehensive treatments for male violence. Educational programs are needed to teach nonviolence and relationship skills to males and to develop more alternatives to the masculine cultural norms of aggression, competition, and exploitation. Instructional courses should be instituted in schools (for young men) and at mental health centers (for adults), much like sex education or birthing classes are conducted.

The diversity of programs for batterers needs to be developed further to create long-term, phased treatment programs. These programs should facilitate the process of change by moving the batterer from jailing to educational classes, to self-help support, to community service—much like the Alcoholics Anonymous scheme. Also, intensive residential programs for multiple-problem and sociopathic batterers need to be established similar to the detoxification centers for alcoholics or residential treatment programs for rapists.

Conclusion

As we stated at the beginning of this book, the shelter movement is facing an increased psychologizing of the abuse problem. A variety of therapies and treatments for women have been devised to help the battered women cope with their victimization and to correct their emotional deficiencies. We have attempted to reemphasize here that, while therapy is certainly appropriate for some women, there is a more urgent agenda at hand. Shelter women, most of all, need resources. They need housing, income, child care, transportation, and education.

Furthermore, it appears from our helpseeking study that the help sources themselves are not adequately responsive. Apparently, women must contact numerous help sources before they obtain some semblance of safety. According to other studies, they often receive insufficient advice or misinformation, and do not receive the resources required to act on good advice when they get it. Moreover, no *one* of the individual help sources is of itself a sufficient intervention.

The shelter movement has undoubtedly made great progress in meeting the crisis of many battered women. What we are confirming here is that shelters cannot alone meet the needs of battered women. The presence of a shelter in a community does not mean that the problem of abuse is taken care of and that other help sources can assume that battered women need not be their priority.

Ultimately, more is needed. Abuse must be seen as a community problem. There needs to be a coordinated and even integrated system of community services and interventions to address abuse. This system needs to respond comprehensively at the point of crisis and to sustain adequate supports over the long term. In this way, battered women might find that reaching out for help is not a frustrating and arduous process but brings prompt, decisive, and realistic assistance. If this were the case, more women would probably be inclined to seek help and to seek it earlier. The helpgiving would therefore be more likely to stop abuse before it escalated, and less additional helpgiving would be required.

Establishing a community-wide response to wife abuse, however, requires more than a neat delivery design or efficient administration. It requires a renewed and heightened awareness of abuse and its consequences. It also requires an increased awareness of the learned helplessness in the help sources. We need to know more of why our help sources have such difficulty giving effective help. Is it simply a matter of funds? Is it more a matter of staffing? Is there sexism or other bias among the helpers?

The more important question is, of course: How do we motivate other help sources to make a commitment to ending abuse? While this book was not intended to fully address this matter, it has attempted to point us back toward a "treatment" of the larger community. We need to treat ourselves much more in order to allow battered women to be survivors. In this way, we will build toward a society free of abuse.

Appendix: Methodology

Procedures

Sampling. Our study of battered women is based on data drawn from shelter intake and exit interviews established by the Texas Council on Family Violence and the Texas Department of Human Services. The sample (N = 6, 612) consists of all those women who entered the fifty Texas shelters during an eighteen-month period in 1984–1985. Those women who were under sixteen years of age and not physically abused (that is, not battered women) were deleted from the final sample (6 percent), along with duplicate and incomplete questionnaires. The incomplete questionnaires (Part Two or Part Three not finished) were from women who were referred elsewhere, or who were from two shelters that did not fully comply with the instructions. The distribution on the general background and abuse questions of Part One of these questionnaires was comparable to the remaining sample. This suggests that the deleted incomplete questionnaires did not particularly bias the results.

Interviews. Shelter staff administered an 84-question interview to each of the shelter women. The questionnaire included questions about three fundamental areas: the woman's background, abuse, and helpseeking. Basic background questions were asked at intake from Part One of the questionnaire. Detailed questions about the nature of the abuse and response to the abuse were asked within three days of the intake from Part Two of the questionnaire. Lastly, questions about shelter services and discharge plans were asked at exit from Part Three of the questionnaire.

The majority of background questions used typical ordinal-level responses about income, education, race, number of children, times married, and so on. The questions about abuse included multiple responses on physical abuse and verbal abuse, and on kind of injury and care sought. Questions about duration and frequency of abuse were ordinal-level responses. The questions relating to previous helpseeking, police action, shelter services obtained, and continued shelter services also allowed for multiple responses. In addition, a variety of dichotomous and categorical response items (such as sexual abuse, batterer in counseling, transportation available) were used throughout the interview questionnaire.

Variables. These questions were transformed into variables for a variety of bivariate and multivariate analyses. The multiple-response questions for abuse and helpseeking were converted into the total number of categories mentioned and also into weighted scores accounting for the rank of the category mentioned. The "total" and "weighted scores" were derived as follows:

First, the categorical responses for a particular question, such as physical abuse or previous helpseeking, were ranked to conform to established scales or the ranking of shelter staff and residents. For example, the question for physical abuse was: "If you were physically abused, which of the following happened? The batterer: (1) threw things, (2) held you against your will, (3) pushed you around, (4) slapped you, (5) pulled your hair, (6) choked you, (7) burned you, (8) punched you, (9) kicked you, (10) used a weapon or object against you." This ranking reflects the ranking of the widely used Conflict Tactics Scale (Straus 1979).

Second, the total number of different categories mentioned by a respondent was calculated and became variable in itself. These "total" variables were quasi-interval and approximated normality; they were therefore used as the basis for our linear multivariate analysis. Representative categorical variables were also inserted in the analysis as dummy variables in order to provide as a check on the quasi-interval variables.

Third, the ranked value of each category was used to calculate a weighted score (the sum of the ranks for the mentioned categories). The weighted score was used in conducting the cluster analysis, for reasons discussed in chapter 5. The "total" for each item was in fact highly correlated with the "weighted scores" ($r > .8$).

Analysis. A variety of multivariate statistical procedures were used to analyze the data. Each chapter includes a brief explanation of the particular statistical procedures employed in analyzing the topic of that chapter. Structural equation modeling was used to develop the causal model that tests the helpseeking hypothesis; discriminate functions were employed to explore the differences in racial groupings, shelter status, police action, and shelter outcome; and a cluster analysis forms the basis of the batterer typology.

Questionnaire Advantages

The comprehensiveness of the questionnaire was particularly beneficial in constructing the analysis. It allowed us to consider several possibilities that were previously unexplored, such as differences in racial groupings, a comparison with shelter nonresidents, and the diversity of batterers. It also enabled us to develop more sophisticated multivariate analyses (structural equation modeling, discriminant functions, and cluster analysis), which have been sorely lacking in the field. Much of the previous shelter-based studies have been largely bivariate (cross-tabulations and simple correlations); they are therefore primarily descriptive rather than explanatory in nature.

The questionnaire additionally provided several measures for one factor. This enabled us to obtain a more valid representation of otherwise difficult and elusive aspects of abuse (see Margolin 1987). We were able to measure, for instance, abuse in terms of physically and verbally abusive behavior as well as in terms of the inflicted injuries and the care they required.

Another advantage to the data base is that it relies entirely on the reporting of the battered women themselves rather than clinician observations, researcher assessments, police reports, shelter records, or batterer accounts, as do several of the other studies on wife abuse. A number of methodological studies have shown that the women's self-reports are the most reliable source of information (Arias and Beach 1987; Barling et al. 1987; Edleson and Brygger 1986; Okum 1986).

There are of course limitations and cautions that accompany these advantages. The efforts to develop measures of severity from what are essentially descriptive categories remains crude, even though they are compensated by corroborating measures and offer a convenient tool for comparisons. Lastly, there are analytical technicalities that inevitably accompany research of this sophistication. These are addressed in various chapter notes.

Sample Comparisons

Another advantage lies in the unusually large sample size and inclusiveness. These serve as a verification for previous shelter studies that have relied on small self-selected samples that could easily be unrepresentative of the larger shelter population. We were able to make statistical comparisons between our sample and other Texas samples and among regional subsamples to better assess the reliability of our sample.[1]

Our Texas shelter data for 1984–85 was contrasted with Texas data from other years. The statistics for each reporting year from 1981–82 to 1985–86 remain relatively constant. We also made regional and urban–rural comparisons for our 1984–85 shelter data. The southern region, as might be expected, was distinguished by a markedly higher proportion of Hispanic women in shelters. The urban areas were typified by more severe abuse.

Yearly. More specifically, a comparison of the five reporting years from 1981 to 1985 showed no statistical difference in minority representation, number of children, education level, and helpseeking.[2] There is evidence of a slight increase in the severity of abuse over the five-year period. The proportion of those reporting being kicked, for instance, increased from 54 percent in 1981 to 56 percent in 1983, 60 percent in 1984, and 59 percent in 1985. Also, the proportion of women reporting weapons used against them rose from 32 percent in 1981 to 41 percent in 1985.

The one outstanding difference was in the unemployment rate for the batterers. The unemployment rate for batterers was 18 percent in 1981 and rose to 34 percent in 1985. This difference was brought on by the recent oil crisis that has depressed the state economy. The effects of this unemployment swing that began in 1985 will no doubt be reflected in more severe abuse in future years, as has been the case in other depressed areas.

Regional. The shelter data for the western, eastern, and southern regions reflects the different demographics of the state.[3] The eastern region (Houston, Dallas, and Austin) had the highest percentage of black shelter residents (22 percent, as opposed to 8 percent in the west and 5 percent in the south). It also registered a higher family income and a higher arrest rate for domestic violence calls.

As might be expected, over half of the shelter women in the southern region (San Antonio, Corpus Christi, and Brownsville) were Hispanic (65 percent, as opposed to 33 percent in the west and 2 percent in the east). The southern region also has lower education and income levels. Fifty-seven percent of the southern shelter women had no high school diploma, whereas 47 percent in the west (El Paso, Amarillo) and 45 percent in the east had not graduated from high school. The implications of the racial differences for abuse and helpseeking are discussed further in chapter 4.

Urban–Rural. Urban (one million+), town (100,000–200,000), and rural (5,000–30,000) areas were also compared.[4] As mentioned, the urban area shelters reported more severe violence than the town and rural areas. For instance, the percentage reporting having been kicked was 64 percent in the urban areas, 52 percent for the town, and 53 percent for rural areas. Weapon use was 43 percent for the urban area and 35 and 32 percent for the town and rural areas, respectively. The helpseeking is correspondingly highest for the urban areas and least for the town. The outstanding difference in the background of shelter women is that the rural areas, as expected, have the smallest minority representation (35 percent black or Hispanic versus 47 percent in the urban areas and 50 percent in the town areas).

Questionnaire (Sample Questions)

The questions used to construct the variables employed in our causal model of helpseeking (see chapter 3) are listed below. These questions are also the principal variables used in other analyses discussed in the book. Other questions used from the interview questionnaire are specifically mentioned in the text. For instance, the question and responses used for "police action" appear in chapter 5 and for "planned living arrangements" in chapter 6. A complete interview questionnaire may be obtained from the Texas Council on Family Violence, 1704 West 6th Street, Suite 200, Austin, Texas 78703.

Background Variables

Victim's Income. Woman's personal income (per year)? (1) none, (2) $0–5,000, $5–10,000, (3) $10–15,000, (4) $15–20,000, (5) $20,000 or more.

Number of Children. The number of children living with the woman during the last six months? 0, 1, 2, 3, 4, 5 or more.

Previous Abuse. (Total of responses to the following—0 = no; 1 = yes.) (1) Were you physically abused as a child? (2) Were you sexually abused as a child? (3) Did your parents have any alcohol-related problems? (4) Did abusive incidents happen between your parents? (5) Were you physically abused in any previous relationship?

Antisocial Behavior

Substance Abuse. (Total of responses to the following—0 = no; 1 = yes.) (1) batterer regularly abuses alcohol (2) or drugs; (3) the physical abuse is generally related to alcohol (4) or drugs; (5) batterer has been arrested for drunken driving (6) or drug possession.

General Violence. Has the batterer been violent toward any of the following? (0) none, (1) objects, (2) your personal belongings, (3) pets or other animals, (4) himself, (5) people outside the home.

Arrests. For what reason has the batterer been arrested? (0) no arrests, (1) public intoxication or DWI, (2) drug possession or use, (3) bad checks or forgery, (4) robbery or theft, (5) child abuse or neglect, (6) violence against the client, (7) violence against others, (8) rape, (9) murder.

Batterer's Response. Immediately after abusive incidents, what has the batterer done? (0) none, (1) apologized, (2) act affectionate, (3) left home, (4) slept or passed out, (5) act as if nothing happened, (6) denied or said didn't hurt you, (7) said you deserve it, (8) made sexual demands, (9) threatened to do it again.

Wife Abuse

Physical Abuse. If you were physically abused, which of the following happened? The batterer: (0) none (1) threw things, (2) held you against your will, (3) pushed you around, (4) slapped you, (5) pulled your hair, (6) choked you, (7) burned you, (8) punched you, (9) kicked you, (10) used a weapon or object against you.

Frequency of Abuse. Within the past six months, how many times have you been abused? (1) only once, (2) once a month or less, (3) two or three times a month, (4) once a week, (5) twice a week to daily.

Verbal Abuse. If you were verbally abused, which of the following happened? (0) none, (1) personal insults, (2) threatened physical harm, (3) threatened sexual abuse, (4) threatened to use weapons, (5) threatened to kill you, (6) threatened to seriously harm your child.

Injury. What type of injuries have you received as a result of the abuse from the current batterer? (0) none, (1) bruises, (2) cuts, (3) sprains, dislocation, (4) teeth knocked out or broken, (5) serious burns, (6) head injury or concussion, (7) broken bones, (8) miscarriage, (9) permanent injury.

Child Abuse

Child Abuse. Have the children been victims of any of the following? (0) none or no children, (1) neglect, (2) verbal or emotional abuse, (3) physical abuse, (4) sexual abuse.

Frequency of Child Abuse. Within the past six months, how often has physical abuse happened? (0) none, (1) only once, (2) once a month or less, (3) two or three times a month, (4) once a week, (5) twice a week to daily.

Helpseeking

Previous Helpseeking. Immediately after abusive incidents, what have you done? (0) nothing, (1) contacted family members, (2) contacted a friend, (3) contacted a clergy person, (4) contacted a social service agency, (5) contacted a shelter, (6) visited a social service agency, (7) threatened batterer, (8) called police, (9) left home, (10) visited a shelter, (11) took legal action.

Notes

1. Cross-tabulations were calculated for the respective groupings (for example, reporting year, region, urban–rural) and the categorical variables. Representative variables with statistically significant differences are reported. For instance, "kicked" or "weapons used" was used to represent the severity of abuse.

2. The comparison is based on the number of shelters reporting during the fiscal year. In 1981–82, 29 of 35 shelters reported; in 1983–84, all of the state's 36 shelters reported; in 1984–85, all 50 shelters reported; and in 1985–86, all 51 shelters in operation comprised the data base. The first reporting year of 1979–80 was excluded from our comparison, since only 15 of 29 shelters reported data at that time.

3. The regions used here are based on geographic divisions established by the Texas Department of Human Services for administrative purposes. The cities in parenthesis are included in the region preceding it, but the particular region is not confined to those cities.

4. The urban–rural categories were designated by the researchers for the purposes of comparison. They represent the two extremes and middle of the continuum of shelter areas. The "urban" category refers to the SMAS areas in the state: Dallas, Houston, and San Antonio, all of which have populations over one million. The "town" category refers to midsized cities such as Abilene, Waco, and Brownsville. The "rural" category refers to the women visiting shelters in Texas small towns separate from any metropolis. Paris, San Marcos, and Nacogdoches are examples of these areas.

References

Abramson, L.Y., M.P. Seligman, and J.D. Teasdale. 1978. "Learned Helplessness in Humans: Critique and Reformulation." *Journal of Abnormal Psychology* 87(1):49–74.

Adams, D. 1986. "Wife Abuse Should be Seen as a Primary Problem, Not a Symptom." *Psychiatric News* 21(11):24–29.

Adrian, M., and C. Mitchell. 1978. *A Study of Spouse Battering in Montana*. Helena, Mont.: Department of Community Affairs.

Aguirre, B.E. 1985. "Why Do They Return? Abused Wives in Shelters." *Social Work* 30:350–354.

Alexson, J., and E. Sinclair. 1986. "Psychiatric Diagnosis and School Placement: A Comparison Between Inpatients and Outpatients." *Child Psychiatry and Human Development* 16(3):194–205.

Arias, I., and S.R. Beach. 1987. "Validity of Self-Reports of Marital Violence." *Journal of Family Violence* 2(2):139–150.

Aschenbrenner, J. 1975. *Lifelines: Black Families in Chicago*. New York: Holt, Rinehart and Winston.

Barling, J., K.D. O'Leary, E. Jouriles, D. Vivan, and K.E. MacEwen. 1987. "Factor Similarity of the Conflict Tactics Scales Across Samples, Spouses, and Sites, Issues and Implications." *Journal of Family Violence* 2(1):37–54.

Bass, D., and J. Rice. 1979. "Agency Responses to the Abused Wife." *Social Casework* 60:338–342.

Berk, R.A., and P.J. Newton. 1986. "Does Arrest Really Deter Wife Battery? An Effort to Replicate the Findings of ;the Minneapolis Spouse Abuse Experiment." *American Sociological Review* 50:253–262.

Berk, R.A., P.J. Newton, and S.F. Berk. 1986. "What a Difference a Day Makes: An Empirical Study of the Impact of Shelters for Battered Women." *Journal of Marriage and the Family* 48:481–490.

Berk, R.A., S.F. Berk, P.J. Newton, and D. Loseke. 1984. "Cops on Call: Summoning the Police to the Scene of Spousal Violence." *Law and Society Review* 18(3):479–498.

Berk, S.F., and D. Loseke. 1980. "Handling Family Violence: Situational Determinants of Police Arrest in Domestic Disturbances." *Law and Society Review* 15(2):317–346.

Bernard, J.L., and M.L. Bernard. 1984. "The Abusive Male Seeking Treatment: Jekyll and Hyde." *Family Relations* 33:543–547.

Bernard, M.L., and J.L. Bernard. 1983. "Violent Intimacy: The Family as a Model for Love Relationships." *Family Relations* 32:283–286.

Bittner, E. 1974. "Florence Nightingale in Pursuit of Willie Sutton: A Theory of Police," in H. Jacob, ed., *The Potential for Reform of Criminal Justice.* Beverly Hills, Calif.: Sage.

Black, D. 1980. *The Manners and Customs of the Police.* New York: Academic.

Block, C. 1981. "Black Americans and the Cross-Cultural Counselling and Psychotherapy Experience." In J. Marsella and P. Pedersen, eds., *Cross-Cultural Counselling and Psychotherapy.* New York: Pergamon.

Borkowski, M., M. Murch, and V. Walker. 1983. *Marital Violence: The Community Response.* New York: Travistock.

Bowker, L.H., 1982. "Police Services to Battered Women: Bad or Not so Bad?" *Criminal Justice and Behavior* 9(4):476–494.

Bowker, L.H. 1983. *Beating Wife Beating.* Lexington, Mass.: Lexington Books.

Bowker, L.H. 1986. *Ending the Violence: A Guidebook Based on the Experiences of 1,000 Battered Wives.* Holmes Beach, Fla.: Learning Publications.

Bowker, L.H., and L. Maurer. 1985. "The Importance of Sheltering in the Lives of Battered Women." *Response* 8(1):2–8.

Browne, A. 1987. *When Battered Women Kill.* New York: Free Press.

Brygger, M.P., and J. Edleson. 1987. "The Domestic Abuse Project: A Multi-Systems Intervention in Woman Battering." *Journal of Interpersonal Violence* 2(2): 324–333.

Byerly, F., and W. Carlson. 1982. "Comparison Among Inpatients, Outpatients, and Normals on Three Self-Report Depression Inventories." *Journal of Clinical Psychology* 38(4):797–804.

Cahalan, D., and R. Room. 1974. *Problem Drinking Among American Men.* New Brunswick, N.J.: Rutgers Center of Alcohol Studies.

Cannon, M., and B. Locke. 1977. "Being Black is Detrimental to One's Mental Health: Myth or Reality?" *Phylon* 38:408–428.

Caplan, P. 1985. *The Myth of Female Masochism.* New York: Dutton.

Cazenave, N.A., and M.A. Straus. 1979. "Race, Class, Network Embeddedness and Family Violence: A Search for Potent Support Systems." *Journal of Comparative Family Studies* 10(3):281–299.

Cuellar, I., L.C. Harries, and R. Jasso. 1980. "An Acculturation Scale for Mexican Normal and Clinical Populations." *Hispanic Journal of Behavioral Sciences* 3:199–271.

Dalton, D., and J. Kantner. 1983. "Aggression in Battered and Nonbattered Women as Reflected in the Hand Test." *Psychological Reports* 53:703–709.

Davies, J.C., ed. 1971. *When Men Revolt—and Why.* New York: Free Press.

Davis, L.V. 1987. "Battered Women: The Transformation of a Social Problem." *Social Work.* 32:306–311.

Deutsch, H. 1944. *The Psychology of Women,* Vol. 1. New York: Grune and Stratton.

Dick, P., L. Cameron, D. Cohen, M. Barlow, and A. Ince. 1985. "Day and Full Time Psychiatric Treatment: A Controlled Comparison." *British Journal of Psychiatry* 147:246–250.

Dobash, E.R., and R. Dobash. 1979. *Violence Against Wives: A Case Against Patriarchy.* New York: Free Press.

Dobash, E.R., and R. Dobash. 1981. "Social Science and Social Action: The Case of Wife Beating." *Journal of Family Issues* 2:27–39.

Dutton, D., and S.L. Painter. 1981. "Traumatic Bonding: The Development of Emotional Attachments in Battered Women and Other Relationships of Intermittent Abuse." *Victimology* 6(1–4):139–155.

Edleson, J.L., and M.P. Brygger. 1986. "Gender Differences in Reporting Battering Incidences." *Family Relations* 35:377–382.

Edleson, J.L., I. Eisikovits, and E. Guttman. 1985. "Men Who Batter Women: A Critical Review of the Evidence." *Journal of Family Issues* 6(2):229–247.

Ehrenreich, B., and D. English. 1979. *For Her Own Good: 150 Years of the Experts' Advice to Women.* Garden City, N.Y.: Anchor.

Elbow, M. 1977. "Theoretical Considerations of Violent Marriages (Personality Characteristics of Wife Abusers)." *Social Casework* 58:515–526.

Erez, Edna. 1986. "Intimacy, Violence, and the Police." *Human Relations* 39(3):265–281.

Evans, L., F. Acosta, J. Yamamoto, and M. Hurwicz. 1986. "Patient Requests: Correlates and Therapeutic Implications for Hispanic, Black and Caucasian Patients." *Journal of Clinical Psychology* 42(1):213–221.

Fagan, J., D. Stewart, and K. Hansen. 1983. "Violent Men or Violent Husbands? Background Factors and Situational Correlates." In D. Finkelhor, R. Gelles, G. Hotaling, and M. Straus, eds., *The Dark Side of Families.* Beverly Hills, Calif.: Sage.

Ferraro, K.J. 1985. "Protecting Women: Police and Battering." Paper presented at the American Sociological Association, Washington, D.C.

Ferraro, K.J. 1983. "Negotiating Trouble in a Battered Women's Shelter." *Urban Life* 12(3):287–306.

Ferraro, K.J., and J.M. Johnson. 1983. "How Women Experience Battering: The Process of Victimization." *Social Problems* 30(3):325–339.

Finkelhor, D. 1984. *Child Sexual Abuse: New Theory and Research.* New York: Free Press.

Fischer, J. 1969. "Negroes and Whites and Rates of Mental Illness: Reconsideration of a Myth." *Psychiatry* 32:428–446.

Frankl, V.E. 1959. *Man's Search for Meaning: An Introduction to Logotherapy.* Boston: Beacon.

Frieze, I.H. 1979. "Perceptions of Battered Wives." In I.H. Frieze, D. Bar-tal, and J.S. Carroll, eds., *New Approaches to Social Problems: Applications of Attribution Theory.* San Francisco: Jossey-Bass.

Frieze, I.H. 1980. "Causal Attributions as Mediators of Battered Women's Responses to Battering." Part of the Final Report to NIMH Grant #1 R01 MH30193, University of Pittsburgh.

Frieze, I.H., J. Knoble, C. Washburn, and G. Zomnir. 1980. "Characteristics of Battered Women and Their Marriages." Part of the Final Report of Grant #1 R01 MH30193, University of Pittsburgh.

Frisbie, W.P. 1986. "Variation in Patterns of Marital Instability among Hispanics." *Journal of Marriage and the Family* 48:99–106.

Gelfand, D., and D. Fandetti. 1986. "The Emergent Nature of Ethnicity: Dilemmas in Assessment." *Social Casework.* 66(4):542–550.

Gelles, R.J. 1976. "Abused Wives: Why Do They Stay?" *Journal of Marriage and the Family* 38(4):659–668.

Gilligan, C. 1982. *In a Different Voice: Psychological Theory and Women's Development.* Cambridge, Mass.: Harvard University Press.

Goldstein, D., and A. Rosenbaum. 1985. "An Evaluation of the Self-Esteem of Maritally Violent Men." *Family Relations* 34:425–428.

Gondolf, E.W. 1984. "Muddling with the Mundane: Social Education Through Group Living." *Small Group Behavior* 15(1):139–152.

Gondolf, E.W. 1985. *Men Who Batter: An Integrated Approach to Stopping Wife Abuse.* Holmes Beach, Fla.: Learning Publications.

Gondolf, E.W. 1987a. "Evaluating Programs for Men Who Batter: Problems and Prospects." *Journal of Family Violence* 2(2):95–108.

Gondolf, E.W. 1987b. "Who Are Those Guys? A Typology of Men Who Batter Based on Shelter Interviews." Paper presented at Third National Family Violence Research Conference, Durham, N.H.

Gondolf, E.W. 1987c. "Changing Men Who Batter: A Developmental Model of Integrated Interventions." *Journal of Family Violence* 2(4):345–369.

Gondolf, E.W. Forthcoming. "Batterer Counseling and Shelter Outcome: An Empirical Study of Planned Living Arrangements." *Journal of Interpersonal Violence.*

Gondolf, E.W. Under review–a. "Handling Antisocial Men: The Police Action in Wife Abuse." *Criminal Justice and Behavior.*

Gondolf, E.W. Under review–b. "Battered Women as Survivors: A Causal Model of Helpseeking." *Journal of Interpersonal Violence.*

Gondolf, E.W., and J. Hanneken. 1987. "The Gender Warrior: Reformed Batterers on Abuse, Treatment, and Change." *Journal of Family Violence* 2(2):177–191.

Gondolf, E.W., E.R. Fisher, and J.R. McFerron. In press. "The Helpseeking Behavior of Battered Women: A Preliminary Analysis of 6,000 Shelter Interviews." *Victimology.*

Gondolf, E.W., E.R. Fisher, and J.R. McFerron. Forthcoming. "Racial Differences Among Shelter Residents: A Comparison of Anglo, Black, and Hispanic Battered Women." *Journal of Family Violence.*

Gondolf, E.W., E.R. Fisher, and J.R. McFerron. Under review. "Shelter Residents and Nonresidents: A Comparative Analysis of Intake Interviews of Battered Women." *Journal of Family Violence.*

Gottlieb, B. 1978. "The Development and Application of a Classification Scheme for Informal Helping Behaviors." *Canadian Journal of Behavioral Science* 10:105–115.

Hamberger, L.K., and J.E. Hastings. 1986. "Personality Correlates of Men Who Abuse Their Partners: A Cross-Validation Study." *Journal of Family Violence* 1(4):323–341.

Hart, B. 1987. *Safety for Women: Monitoring Batterers Programs.* Harrisburg, Pa.: Pennsylvania Coalition Against Domestic Violence.

Higgins, J.G. 1978. "Social Services for Abused Wives." *Social Casework* 59:266–271.

Hotaling, G.T., and D . Sugarman, 1986. "An Analysis of Risk Makers in Husband to Wife Violence: The Current State of Knowledge." *Violence and Victims* 1(2):101–124.

Janoff–Bulman, R., and I. Frieze. 1983. "A Theoretical Perspective for Understanding Reactions to Victimization." *Journal of Social Issues* 39(2):1–17.

Jessor, R., T. Graves, R. Hanson, and S. Jessor. 1968. *Society, Personality, and Deviant Behavior*. New York: Holt, Rinehart, and Winston.

Johnson, J.M. 1981. "Program Enterprise and Official Cooptation in the Battered Shelter Movement." *American Behavioral Scientist* 24(6):827–842.

Joreskog, K.G., and D. Sorbom. 1986. *LISREL VI: Analysis of Linear Structural Relations by Maximum Likelihood, Instrumental Variables, and Least Squares Methods*. Mooresville, Ind.: International Educational Services.

Kalmuss, D.S. 1984. "The Intergenerational Transmission of Marital Aggression." *Journal of Marriage and the Family* 47(1):11–19.

Kalmuss, D.S., and M.A. Straus. 1982. "Wife's Marital Dependency and Wife Abuse." *Journal of Marriage and the Family* 44:277–286.

Keefe, S. 1982. "Help-Seeking Behavior Among Foreign-Born and Native-Born Mexican Americans." *Social Science and Medicine* 16:1467–1472.

Kern, J., W. Schmelter, and M. Fanelli. 1978. "A Comparison of Three Alcoholism Treatment Populations: Implications for Treatment." *Journal of Studies on Alcohol* 39(5):785–793.

Kiley, D. 1983. *The Peter Pan Syndrome: Men Who Never Grow Up*. New York: Dodd, Mead.

Kleckner, J. 1978. "Wife Beaters and Beaten Wives: Co-Conspirators in Crimes of Violence." *Psychology* 15:54–56.

Kravits, J., and J. Schneider. 1975. "Health Care Need and Actual Use by Age, Race, and Income." In R. Anderson, J. Kravits, and O. Anderson, eds., *Equity in Health Services*. Cambridge, Mass.: Ballinger.

Kurz, D. 1987. "Emergency Department Responses to Battered Women: Resistance to Medicalization." *Social Problems* 34(1):69–81.

Lantz, H. 1972. *A Community in Search of Itself*. Carbondale, Ill.: Southern Illinois University Press.

Lazare, A., S. Eisenthal, L. Wasserman, and T. Harford. 1975. "Patient Requests in Walk-In Clinic." *Comprehensive Psychiatry* 16:467–477.

Lenz, E., and B. Myerhoff. 1985. *The Feminization of America: How Women's Values Are Changing Our Public and Private Lives*. New York: St. Martin's.

Lifton, R.J. *Death in Life: Survivors of Hiroshima*. New York: Random House.

Loseke, D.R., and S.F. Berk. 1982. "The Work of Shelters: Battered Women and Initial Calls for Help." *Victimology* 7:35–48.

Margolin. G. 1987. "The Multiple Forms of Aggressiveness Between Marital Partners: How Do We Identify Them?" *Journal of Marital and Family Therapy* 13(1):77–84.

Martin, D. 1976. *Battered Wives*. San Francisco: Glide.

McAdoo, H. 1978. "Factors Related to Stability in Upwardly Mobile Black Families." *Journal of Marriage and the Family* 40:762–778.

McEvoy, A., J.B. Brookings, and C.E. Brown. 1983. "Responses to Battered Women: Problems and Strategies." *Social Work* 27:92–96.

McKinlay, J. 1975. "The Help Seeking Behavior of the Poor." In J. Kosa and I. Zola, eds., *Poverty and Health: A Sociological Analysis* (2nd ed.). Cambridge, Mass.: Harvard University Press.

McShane, C. 1979. "Community Services for Battered Women." *Social Work* 23:34–39.

Mills, T. 1985. "The Assault on the Self: Stages in Coping with Battering Husbands." *Qualitative Sociology* 8(2):103–123.

Mitchell, R.E., and C.A. Hodson. 1983. "Coping with Domestic Violence: Social Support and Psychological Health Among Battered Women." *American Journal of Community Psychology* 11(6):629–654.

Neidig, P.N., D.H. Friedman, and B.S. Collins. 1986. "Attitudinal Characteristics of Males Who Have Engaged in Spouse Abuse." *Journal of Family Violence* 1(3):223–234.

Neighbors, H. 1984. "Professional Help Use Among Black Americans: Implications for Unmet Need." *American Journal of Community Psychology* 12(5):551–565.

Neighbors, H., and J. Jackson. 1984. "The Use of Informal and Formal Help: Four Patterns of Illness Behavior in the Black Community." *American Journal of Community Psychology* 12(6):629–644.

NiCarthy, G. 1986. *Getting Free: A Handbook for Women in Abusive Relationships.* Seattle, Wash.: Seal Press.

Oberschall, A. 1973. *Social Conflict and Social Movements.* Englewood Cliffs, N.J.: Prentice–Hall.

Okum, L. 1986. *Woman Abuse: Facts Replacing Myths.* Albany, N.Y.: State University of New York Press.

Pagelow, M.D. 1981. *Woman-battering: Victims and Their Experiences.* Beverly Hills, Calif.: Sage.

Pagelow, M.D. 1984. *Family Violence.* New York: Praeger.

Penk, W.E., H.L. Charles, and T.A. Van Hoose. 1979. "Psychological Test Comparison of Day Hospital and Inpatient Treatment." *Journal of Clinical Psychology* 35(4):837–839.

Petersen, R. 1980. "Social Class, Social Learning, and Wife Abuse." *Social Service Review* 53:390–406.

Pfouts, J.S. 1978. "Violent Families: Coping Responses of Abused Wives." *Child Welfare* 57:101–111.

Phelps, S., and N. Austin. 1975. *The Assertive Woman.* San Luis Obispo, Calif.: Impact Publishers.

Pleck, E. 1987. *Domestic Tyranny: The Making of American Social Policy Against Family Violence From Colonial Times to the Present.* New York: Oxford University Press.

Priog–Good, M., and J. Stets–Kealey. 1986. "Programs for Abusers: Who Drops Out and What Can Be Done." *Response* 9(2):17–19.

Rieker, P.P., and E.H. Carmen. 1986. "The Victim-to-Patient Process: The Disconfirmation and Transformation of Abuse." *American Journal of Orthopsychiatry* 56(3):360–370.

Rosenbaum, A. 1986. "Of Men, Macho, and Marital Violence." *Journal of Family Violence* 1(2):121–130.

Rosenbaum, A., and K.D. O'Leary. 1981. "Marital Violence: Characteristics of Abusive Couples." *Journal of Consulting and Clinical Psychology* 49:63–71.

Saunders, D.G. 1986. "When Battered Women Use Violence: Husband-Abuse and Self-Defense." *Violence and Victims* 1(1):47–60.

Schechter, S. 1982. *Women and Male Violence: The Visions and Struggles of the Battered Women's Movement.* Boston: South End Press.

Schrumm, W.R., J.J. Martin, S.R. Bolman, and A.P. Jurich. 1982. "Classifying Family Violence: Wither the Woozle." *Journal of Family Issues* 3(3):319–340.

Schulman, M.A. 1979. *A Survey of Spousal Violence Against Women in Kentucky.* Lexington: Kentucky Commission on Women.

Seligman, M.E.P. 1975. *Helplessness: On Depression, Development, and Death.* San Francisco: W.H. Freeman.

Seligman, M.E.P., and S.F. Maier. 1967. "Failure to Escape Traumatic Shock." *Journal of Experimental Psychology* 74:1–9.

Shainess, N. 1979. "Vulnerability to Violence: Masochism as a Process." *American Journal of Psychotherapy* 33:174–189.

Shainess, N. 1984. *Sweet Suffering: Woman as Victim.* New York: Bobbs–Merrill.

Sherman, L., and R. Berk. 1984. "The Deterrent Effects of Arrest for Domestic Assault." *American Sociological Review* 49(2):261–272.

Shields, N.M., and C.R. Hanneke. 1983. "Violent Husbands: Patterns of Individual Violence." Unpublished report presented to NIMH.

Sidel, R. 1986. *Women and Children Last: The Plight of Poor Women in Affluent America.* New York: Viking.

Skinner, H. 1981. "Comparison of Clients Assigned to Inpatient and Outpatient Treatment for Alcoholism and Drug Addiction." *British Journal of Psychiatry* 138:312–320.

Snell, J., R. Rosenwald, and A. Rokey. 1964. "The Wifebeater's Wife." *Archives of General Psychiatry* 11:109–114.

Snyder, D.K., and L.A. Fruchtman. 1981. "Differential Patterns of Wife Abuse: A Data-Based Typology." *Journal of Consulting and Clinical Psychology* 49(6):878–885.

Snyder, D.K., and N.S. Scheer. 1981. "Predicting Disposition Following Brief Residence at a Shelter for Battered Women." *American Journal of Community Psychology* 9(5):559–566.

Stacey, W.A., and A. Shupe. 1983. *The Family Secret: Domestic Violence in America.* Boston: Beacon.

Stack, C. 1974. *All Our Kin: Strategies for Survival in the Black Community.* New York: Harper and Row.

Stark, E., A. Flitcraft, and W. Frazier. 1979. "Medicine and Patriarchal Violence: the Social Construction of a 'Private' Event." *International Journal of Health Services* 9:461–493.

Steinem, G. 1983. *Outrageous Acts and Everday Rebellions.* New York: Holt, Rinehart and Winston.

Stith, Sandra. 1987. "Individual and Family Factors Which Predict Policy Response to Spouse Abuse." Paper presented at the Third National Family Violence Research Conference, Durham, N.H.

Straus, M., R. Gelles, and S. Steinmetz. 1980. *Behind Closed Doors: Violence in the American Family.* New York: Anchor/Doubleday.

Straus, Murray. 1979. "Measuring Intrafamily Conflict and Violence: The Conflict Tactics (CT) Scales." *Journal of Marriage and the Family* 41:75–78.

Strube, M.J., and L.S. Barbour. 1983. "The Decision to Leave an Abusive Relationship: Economic Dependence and Psychological Commitment." *Journal of Marriage and the Family* 45:785–793.

Taylor, R. 1986. "Receipt of Support from Family among Black Americans: Demographic and Familial Differences." *Journal of Marriage and the Family* 48:67–77.

Tavris, C., and C. Wade. 1984. *The Longest War: Sex Differences in Perspective* (2nd ed.). New York: Harcourt Brace Jovanovich.

Teske, R., and M.L. Parker. 1983. "Spouse Abuse in Texas: A Study of Women's Attitudes and Experiences." Criminal Justice Center Publication, Sam Houston State University, Huntsville, Texas.

Tierney, K.J. 1982. "The Battered Women Movement and the Creation of the Wife Beating Problem." *Social Problems* 29(3):207–220.

Torres, S. In press. "A Comparative Analysis of Wife Abuse Among Anglo-American and Mexican–American Battered Women: Attitudes, Nature and Extent, and Response to the Abuse." *Victimology.*

Turner, S.F., and C.H. Shapiro. 1986. "Battered Women: Mourning the Death of a Relationship." *Social Work* 30:372–376.

U.S. Department of Housing and Urban Development. 1987. "Center for Battered Women and Austin Apartment Association Transitional Housing Program." In *Official U.S. Special Merit Award Projects: International Year of Shelter for the Homeless.* Washington, D.C.: U.S. Department of Housing and Urban Development.

Walker, L. 1979. *The Battered Woman.* New York: Harper and Row.

Walker, L. 1984. *The Battered Woman Syndrome.* New York: Springer.

Warren, D. 1981. *Helping Networks: How People Cope with Problems in the Urban Community.* Notre Dame, Ind.: University of Notre Dame Press.

Washburn, C., and I.H. Frieze. 1980. "Methodological Issues in Studying Battered Women." Paper presented at the Annual Research Conference of the Association for Women in Psychology, Santa Monica, Calif.

Washburn, S., M. Vannicelli, R. Longabaugh, and B.J. Scheff. 1976. "A Controlled Comparison of Psychiatric Day Treatment and Inpatient Hospitalization." *Journal of Consulting and Clinical Psychology* 44(4):665–675.

Webster, J. 1973. *The Realities of Police Work.* Des Moines, Iowa: Kendell/Hunt.

Weingourt, R. 1985. "Never to be Alone: Existential Therapy with Battered Women." *Journal of Psychosocial Nursing* 23(3):24–29.

Werner, E., and R. Smith. 1982. *Vulnerable But Invincible: A Study of Resilient Children.* New York: McGraw–Hill.

White, E.C. 1985. *Chain, Chain, Change.* Seattle, Wash.: Seal Press.

Wood, W., and S. Sherrets. 1984. "Requests for Outpatient Mental Health Services: A Comparison of Whites and Blacks." *Comprehensive Psychiatry* 25(3):329–334.

Worden, R., and A. Pollitz. 1984. "Police Arrests in Domestic Disturbances: A Further Look." *Law and Society Review* 18(1):105–119.

Yllo, K. 1983. "Sexual Equality and Violence Against Wives in American States." *Journal of Comparative Family Studies* 14(1):67–86.

Index

About the Authors

Edward W. Gondolf, Ed.D., is a research fellow at the Western Psychiatric Institute and Clinic of the University of Pittsburgh, and a professor of sociology at Indiana University of Pennsylvania (IUP). He has also worked as a group counselor for the Second Step program for men who batter in Pittsburgh. Dr. Gondolf is the author of *Men Who Batter: An Integrated Approach to Stopping Wife Abuse* (1985), *Man-to-Man: A Guide for Men in Abusive Relationships* (1987), *Research on Men Who Batter: An Overview, Bibliography, and Resource Guide* (1988), and *Staying Stopped: A Gender-Based Workbook for Changing Abusive Men* (1988), as well as numerous research articles on men who batter and on community development.

Ellen Rubenstein Fisher, M.S.W., is the executive director of the Austin Center for Battered Women and board member of the Texas Council on Family Violence. She has previously worked as the Family Violence Program Specialist of the Texas Department of Human Services and as one of the founders of the Austin Rape Crisis Center. The Austin Center for Battered Women, under Ms. Fisher's direction, was honored as a Special Merit Project by the U.S. Department of Housing and Urban Development. The Center has also been designated a Distinguished Victims Services Program by the National Organization for Victims Assistance.